"As someone who grew up [...] questions about infant baptism, I wish I could have read [...] book years ago. McKnight has given the church an enduring gift—a book that is theologically rich, serious, and steeped in tradition yet accessible and readable. As a mother of young children and as a priest, I will put this book in the hands of many a friend and parishioner. If you are a parent deciding whether to baptize infant children, this book is essential reading."

—**Tish Harrison Warren**, priest in the ACNA, co-associate rector (Church of the Ascension Pittsburgh), and author of *Liturgy of the Ordinary: Sacred Practices in Everyday Life*

"Able, strong, wise, and biblically and theologically rich—that's pretty much the case with anything Scot McKnight writes. And here he goes again, this time on the subject of infant baptism. There are a great number of confusions and misunderstandings about infant baptism that Scot thoughtfully clarifies. So even if you don't end up being convinced, you will know why people like Scot (and me) think it is a practice essential for proper Christian discipleship."

—**Mark Galli**, editor in chief, *Christianity Today*

"Scot McKnight provides a controversial though ultimately compelling case for infant baptism. He narrates his own journey from previously holding to believer's baptism as an Anabaptist to now settling on infant baptism as an Anglican. McKnight offers here a robust biblical defense of infant baptism. But it is not just the who and how of baptism that he tackles; the genius of this book is that McKnight elegantly explains what baptism is even about, what it means, what it does for the recipient, and why it really does take a church to baptize a child. Read it with caution: this book could change your whole view of conversion, faith, family, children's ministry, and the church!"

—**Michael F. Bird**, Ridley College, Melbourne, Australia

"In *It Takes a Church to Baptize*, Scot McKnight offers the most compelling case for infant baptism available today. Not content to sprinkle with prooftexts, McKnight immerses his reader in the biblical, historical, and sacramental theology of this ancient Christian practice, and seals it with a testimony of how his mind was changed. Read this book—and remember your baptism!"

—**Joel Scandrett**, Robert E. Webber Center,
Trinity School for Ministry

"Somebody has needed to write this book for some time, but maybe we were waiting for Scot McKnight. *It Takes a Church to Baptize* is just the right prescription for many Christians drawn to more deeply rooted expressions of the Christian faith but facing an obstacle of conscience: 'Yes, eventually the church came to baptize infants, but can such a practice possibly be biblical? What, if anything, does that action actually accomplish—or does it merely signify?' Having been on this journey himself, McKnight offers a more-than-biblical account of these and other questions, not merely with a scorecard of exegetical skirmishes but with a holistic biblical theology rendering the people of God and rehearsing the actions of a saving God. This finally will be the book I recommend to Christians asking these questions."

—**Garwood P. Anderson**, Nashotah House
Theological Seminary

IT TAKES A
CHURCH
TO BAPTIZE

WHAT THE BIBLE SAYS
ABOUT *INFANT* BAPTISM

SCOT McKNIGHT

BrazosPress

a division of Baker Publishing Group
Grand Rapids, Michigan

Published by Brazos Press
a division of Baker Publishing Group
PO Box 6287, Grand Rapids, MI 49516-6287
www.brazospress.com

Printed in the United States of America

Library of Congress Cataloging-in-Publication Data
Names: McKnight, Scot, author.
Title: It takes a church to baptize : what the Bible says about infant baptism / Scot McKnight.
Description: Grand Rapids : Baker Publishing Group, 2018. | Includes bibliographical references and index.
Identifiers: LCCN 2017052471 | ISBN 9781587434167 (pbk. : alk. paper)
Subjects: LCSH: Infant baptism.
Classification: LCC BV813.3 .M39 2018 | DDC 234/.1612—dc23
LC record available at https://lccn.loc.gov/2017052471

Scripture quotations are from the Holy Bible, New International Version®. NIV®. Copyright © 1973, 1978, 1984, 2011 by Biblica, Inc.™ Used by permission of Zondervan. All rights reserved worldwide. www.zondervan.com

18   19   20   21   22   23   24   7   6   5   4   3   2   1

To those who, like the Bereans of Paul's mission,
with "noble character" open their Bibles
and "examine the Scriptures every day
to see if what . . . is said is true.
As a result, many of them believe."
(based on Acts 17:11–12)

Contents

Foreword

In 1979 I was a young church planter in a city that seemed full of young, lapsed Catholics. I can't remember exactly what the young girl had done (premarital sex? underage drinking? experimenting with drugs?), but I'll never forget her ethnic Catholic mom, tears running down her face, screaming at her through a cry-choked voice: *How could you do that? You were baptized!*

That moment played right into and vindicated my then-existing bias that infant baptism was a dead, or at best rote, religious ceremony that accomplished nothing—similar to marriage vows that commonly end in divorce. It also reinforced my fear that infant baptism did not normally lead to personal and real salvation.

Setting aside Catholics and mainline Protestants for a moment, it is true that mid-twentieth-century evangelicals also deserve criticism for their own faults regarding salvation and discipleship. But even so, who could blame us, looking at the state of the mainline churches in the 1960s and 1970s that practiced infant baptism, for wondering what good it did? It seemed one could more easily draw a correlation between infant

baptism and unfaithfulness—between infant baptism and mil-
lions of crying, yelling parents!

Into this picture comes the valuable voice of my friend and
colleague Scot. He offers a corrective by saying *it takes a church
community* and a family—sponsors, godparents, and a praying
congregation—to baptize well.

But as a young evangelical, I strongly believed the opposite: baptism was a sign of a previous moment of salvation,
and furthermore, it was precisely a *personal* decision to follow
the command of Jesus and the biblical norm to be baptized.
Baptism, in its essence, had only to do with me and God. We
"went forward" down the aisle to get saved as *individuals*, not
as families, not even as groups of friends. We were unapologeti-
cally dissing the (usually mainline) church of our families! There
were people standing around the pool when I was rebaptized as
an adult, but they were bystanders (loving as they might have
been), peripheral to what was centrally happening between me
and God. Or so I thought . . .

Coming forward to today, I am often asked about my journey
from the Jesus Movement (Calvary Chapel) and the charismatic
stream of evangelicalism (the Vineyard) to the sacramental part
of the church—specifically, the Anglican Church in North
America. Inevitably, as part of that conversation, a person will
ask: How, given your background with infant dedication and
adult baptism, did you come to believe in and practice infant
baptism? I must confess that, as I considered entering the Anglican community and surveyed the theological landscape of
Anglicanism, I had only one big theological issue to process,
and it was that precise subject: infant baptism.

For me, the other, more visible aspects of Anglican worship such as styles of liturgy, churchmanship, vestments, or
other outward practices were not make-or-break issues. I could

warmly accept and celebrate any approach to church that helped people come to and grow in Christ. But I was still left, to cite the election of 2000, with that theological "hanging chad" of infant baptism.

Fortunately, my reexamination of infant baptism occurred in the context of a long experience that demonstrated to me that Anglican theology is right-down-the-middle historic orthodoxy—beautifully so, in many cases. As a young Jesus Movement evangelical in the 1970s, my favorite authors included Anglicans such as C. S. Lewis, J. I. Packer, and John Stott—pillars of everything intelligent, loving, solid, and godly, right? Later I discovered other trusted and revered Anglican scholars such as Tom Wright and Scot McKnight, who *spoke my language* and thus made great sense to me.

These infant baptizers convinced me of several things:

1. **Theologically:** When viewed in the context of covenant theology and community rather than twentieth-century individualistic reductions of soteriology, infant baptism makes sense.

2. **Biblically:** The relevant Bible texts (with which Scot deals so well) at least allow for, surely suggest, and maybe even insist on infant baptism.

3. **Historically:** The largest part of the Christian church over all times and places has practiced infant baptism.

4. **Personally:** As part of a culturally Christian family, I was baptized as a child in a United Methodist Church. Later, at rebaptism, I was definitely saying something public: *this is my first step in following Jesus.* I saw it as initiation, obedience, and identification with Jesus, his people, and the movement he gave birth to and was bringing to its fulfillment. I now see infant baptism, when practiced

in the manner Scot articulates, to be capable of carrying that same freight.

That's my story—and I hope it helps you get ready to read *It Takes a Church to Baptize.*

Scot McKnight is a careful thinker and a lover of God, church, and Scripture. The vision he casts for the practice of baptism comes from and is wrapped up in those loves. His work in this book has the potential to have next-generation parents joyfully testifying: *Of course you followed Jesus—you were baptized!*

Todd D. Hunter
Anglican bishop, Churches for the Sake of Others

Preface

A LETTER

I get letters like the one below from Matt often. If it is not a letter, it is a question addressed to me by students, friends, pastors, or those who approach me after speaking somewhere. Those who believe baptism is for believers only upon profession of personal faith struggle with those who believe in baptizing infants.* This letter expresses the heart of the question.

Dear Scot,

Greetings!

By way of introduction my name is Matt and I am an Anglican Priest in the ACNA. I have been a fan of your blog and podcast for some time. I had a question that I thought perhaps you might have some insight into. As someone who became Anglican yourself and as a New

---

* Some call those who believe in baptism upon profession of faith "credo-baptists," while infant baptizers are sometimes called "paedo-baptists," with "paedo" meaning child or infant.

Testament scholar, how do you explain infant baptism to someone who comes from a tradition that baptizes adults only?

When I try to explain it to others, I approach it from the belief that it can be logically inferred based on a canonical reading of scripture as a whole, but that doesn't always fare well with the "show me from the Bible crowd." Related to that, how do you explain what happens at infant baptism?

As an Anglican obviously you know our baptismal liturgy is heavy with the language of regeneration and being born again through the waters of baptism. How do you put to ease, if you will, people who are worried such language excludes a person from having to profess personal faith?

I know that's quite a question to answer via email. If you have any articles or blog posts you can point me to that would be fine as well. God's continual blessing on your ministry. It has certainly helped me!

Matt[1]

This book seeks to answer the question Matt asks, as well as some of the questions behind his question. I have my eye especially on the many today who are attracted to the Anglican Church, to *The Book of Common Prayer* and its beautiful prayers or "collects," to the lectionary approach to Sunday worship, and to the liturgical ordering of the church calendar, but who *deep in their hearts* are not convinced the Bible teaches infant baptism and who worry that baptizing infants may diminish the importance of personal conversion. Many of them will join in chorus those whom Michael Green, a New Testament scholar and Anglican bishop, had in mind when he wrote these words about what concerned them about infant baptism: "The answer of the Baptists, the Open Brethren, and many of the House Churches in Britain and fast-growing independent churches overseas is that there is no adequate ground for baptizing infants. It is a scandal. It makes for gross nominalism. It inoculates people against the gospel by making them think that they are Christians when they may be nothing of the kind."[2]

What Michael Green says about concerns in the United Kingdom is even more true in the United States. As the mainline continues its decline, those words may be even more true today than when Green wrote them. Many of us know those baptized as infants who don't follow Christ, many know others who came to Christ later and eschewed their infant baptism and were baptized by immersion, and many want to know how one can with a straight face believe that the Bible actually teaches infant baptism.

It's the right time to say, "Don't throw out the baby with the baptismal waters."

~~~

I am grateful to a number of fellow Anglicans who read *It Takes a Church to Baptize* in its various versions, including my pastor, Jay Greener, as well as Ethan McCarthy, Gerald McDermott, Todd Hunter, Dennis Okholm, John Armstrong, Garwood Anderson, and Mike Bird. I am grateful for their feedback, corrections, criticisms, and suggestions, many of which have found their way into this book. In the process of putting these thoughts into a book, I discovered more emphatically that there is considerable variety in the Anglican Communion, with some leaning toward evangelicalism (as I do) and others leaning toward Anglo-Catholicism, and with plenty at various locations along that spectrum.

Our Baptism

FIRST SIX WORDS

Perhaps you are like me. I grew up Baptist and have been baptistic in my view of baptism for most of my life. To be baptistic is to believe that only believers should be baptized, by full immersion into a pool of water, and that baptizing infants by sprinkling or pouring is wrong. Strange as it may seem, reading the Bible led me on a long and winding road to embrace infant baptism as the view most consistent with the Bible. Many have gone before me on this path, and perhaps you are wondering whether this is the path for you. This book, I hope, approaches this topic in the spirit of civility as it offers a biblical case for infant baptism surrounded by both family and church. I write this book for you and your children and for our church. Infant baptism is the first public step in nurturing our children into the faith.[1]

You may be surprised by that statement. Perhaps you have heard, as I did as a child, that liberal churches baptize infants—and look at their numbers. Their churches are dwindling annually. You may have heard that children who grow up with baptism behind them have not genuinely experienced their baptism, and you may have heard that infant baptism automatically places a child in the church and that child then never has to respond to the gospel. Every one of those concerns is of value to me because I held each one of them and changed my mind. *It Takes a Church to Baptize* will provide reasons from the Bible for infant baptism. So if you are doubtful or wondering, I invite you to reconsider infant baptism for its power to nurture your children into the faith.

First Word: Family

The nucleus of a church is the family, and "family" includes a single-person family as well as families with bundles of little children running around. Pastors and leaders in churches are vital, but the health of the church is shaped by healthy families. Nurturing children into the faith, therefore—whether by family instruction, Sunday school formation, preaching, teaching, or catechism—is the lifeblood of spiritual formation. Children do not grow into the faith by accident. It has been said that more is "caught than taught," but what is "caught" has no value without the "taught." The location of infant baptism in the church is the family because it is families—moms and dads—who bring their children to the church's leaders for baptism.

This matters to me because, now in my sixties, I walk with my grandson, Aksel, and my granddaughter, Finley, together with Kris and those grandchildren's parents, Lukas and Annika, forward to the Communion table on most Sundays. I think about them often when I am listening to and watching our priest, Jay Greener, or our curate, Amanda Holm Rosengren, as they are saying what they say and doing what they do. Each action in our service *embodies* something valuable in the gospel we preach and seek to live. As they are doing pastoral duties up front, Jay and Susan Greener's grandsons are often watching, and Amanda and Erik's daughter, Ruthie, is almost at the age where she will be watching her mom. What is the best way to form our children into the faith? What is the deepest way to nurture them into the faith? The family, beginning with their entrance into the church through baptism.

Infant baptism is one of those acts Jay and Amanda perform among us, and to our delight, we have many little kids in our church. We have participated in the baptism of most of them. As I watch Jay and Amanda perform a baptism, all kinds of theological wheels turn in my head, and I wanted to put them all down in a book to help people like me—those who grew up believing only in baptism upon confession of faith—to see why it is that we baptize our babies.

It Takes a Church to Baptize will walk us through what we are doing and the commitments we as a church are making. I hope this book will show you that infant baptism is the deepest, wisest, and most historic Christian way of forming our children into the faith. Infant baptism begins with the family and extends to the spiritual family, the church. Dietrich Bonhoeffer, in his stunningly influential *Discipleship*, brought baptism's deepest meaning to the surface when he said, "With regard to infant baptism this means that the sacrament should be administered *only where it is certain that the act of salvation already accomplished once and for all will be repeatedly remembered in faith*. And that can only be the case *in a living church-community*. Infant baptism *without the church-community* is not only an abuse of the sacrament. It also betrays a reprehensible thoughtlessness in dealing with the children's spiritual welfare, for baptism can never be repeated."[2] *It Takes a Church to Baptize* affirms these words by Dietrich Bonhoeffer and seeks to show why: to baptize an infant apart from family spiritual formation and apart from a church that nurtures and educates its youth into spiritual maturity violates what baptism means.

So important is the family to baptism that I toyed with titling this book *It Takes a Family to Baptize*. If readers would immediately think by "family" I mean both the birth family and the spiritual family (the church in a local setting) as well as singles, who are too often excluded in churches and for whom the word "family" is experienced as a form of exclusion, that title would say all that needs to be said.

Second Word: Bible

I am a Bible guy who agrees with what Presbyterian theologian and church leader Bryan Chapell once wrote in his booklet on infant baptism: "Biblically minded Christians rightly want to see scriptural confirmation of their churches' practices."[3] More often than not when the subject of infant baptism comes up I am asked, "Does the Bible teach infant baptism?" I agree that we must begin with the Bible, and I too want to see scriptural confirmations, but that means at least one honest admission. Right up front I admit there is no text in the New Testament that explicitly reveals the *practice* of infant baptism in the apostolic church.[4] No text in the New Testament ever says explicitly, "So Paul baptized Publius's three-day-old daughter Junia." Honest admission given, but if you stick with me you will see that the early church did baptize infants and that the New Testament witnesses to that practice. Infant baptism may not be explicit, but it is implicit, and it is implicit far more often than some think.

It is also to be admitted that the New Testament's evidence, from the Gospels on into the apostolic writings, witnesses to *adults* repenting and being baptized in the name of Jesus and in the name of the Father, Son, and Holy Spirit. To be admitted, too, is that those baptisms were most likely by way of immersion.[5] Where does that leave the baptism of infants for the one who is constrained by Scripture? I will devote chapter 5 to answering this question, but at this point this must be said: there may be no explicit account of an infant being baptized, but infant baptism *is* implicit in household baptisms that occurred in the context of early house churches.[6] Even more, if the explicit practice of infant baptism may not be present in the New Testament, a *theology* for infant baptism is to be found already in the new covenant, as baptism correlates with the role of circumcision in the old covenant. That theology is profoundly based in the Bible itself.

I want to mention some of the big ideas from the Bible at work in this theology that leads us to infant baptism. We will take a look later in this book at specific Bible verses used to defend infant baptism, verses such as Colossians 2:11–12 along with 1 Corinthians 7:14.[7] Before we get to those verses, however, I want say a bit more about a theology of infant baptism. Infant baptism makes sense because of big ideas in the Bible. The Bible's big ideas include covenant, sin, and ritual, as well as forgiveness and salvation.

Two of the Bible's big ideas can be discussed here very briefly, beginning with ritual. The word "ritual" may make many of us nervous, but ritual has played an important role in human history.[8] We mark transitions in life by rituals—births and deaths, marriages and divorces, graduations from schools, initiations into a new career, celebrations for accomplishments, and one sports event after another with rituals from trophy ceremonies to commemorations of great athletic feats. I could go on but won't. What needs to be said is that there is something profoundly human about marking major transition events and life accomplishments with some kind of ritual. Ritual and religion go hand in hand because ritual and life go hand in hand. In the Bible itself, ancient Israelites marked the birth of a male child with circumcision, they marked the glory of liberation at the exodus with an annual feast with a variety of rituals, and they created a calendar so no one would ever forget the redemption of God in their midst. How did they celebrate those events of redemption? With rituals. Infant baptism, like circumcision among Jews, fits in the common rituals of life. It is no surprise then that the Bible itself affirms rituals.

Now the second big idea in a theology of infant baptism. The Bible verses that connect the ritual of baptism with *redemption* itself are sometimes ignored, but the apostles could not have imagined salvation apart from the ritual of baptism. Only those of us who have diminished the importance of religious rituals, while preserving them everywhere else in culture, wonder why verses such as Acts 2:38, Galatians 3:27, and 1 Peter 3:21 connect the ritual of baptism so tightly with salvation itself.[9] To get us all thinking about how the Bible connects the ritual of baptism and salvation, here are the texts of those verses:

> Peter replied, "Repent and be baptized, every one of you, in the name of Jesus Christ *for the forgiveness of your sins*. And you will receive the gift of the Holy Spirit." (Acts 2:38)

> For all of you who were baptized into Christ *have clothed yourselves with Christ*. (Gal. 3:27)

> And this water symbolizes *baptism that now saves you also*— not the removal of dirt from the body but the pledge of a clear conscience toward God. It saves you by the resurrection of Jesus Christ. (1 Pet. 3:21)

These big ideas at work in a theology of infant baptism have led the majority of the church through almost its entire history to embrace infant baptism. We learn these big ideas in the Bible.

Third Word: Gospel

We need to avoid misunderstanding baptism, cheapening it by thinking it is magical or demeaning it by not letting the Bible say what it really does say about baptism. The priority of Paul's words that "Christ did not send me to baptize, but to preach the gospel" (1 Cor. 1:17) should be our priority too: first the gospel, with baptism as the enactment of the gospel. Baptism is not the gospel, but the gospel is presented in baptism, and the gospel is embodied in baptism. Baptism is a public act that pronounces to the world something God has done for us.

What is the gospel?[10] The gospel is the announcement of the good news that God has sent his Son, King Jesus, to rule the world. His Son was sent to become like us—a human—so he could usher us into the presence of God as fully accepted. The apostle Paul explicitly defines the gospel in his first letter to the Corinthians when he says, "For what I received I passed on to you as of first importance: that Christ died for our sins according to the Scriptures, that he was buried, that he was raised on the third day according to the Scriptures, and that he appeared to Cephas, and then to the Twelve" (15:3–5).

The gospel then is to tell the story of Jesus in such a way that it fulfills the story of Israel in the Old Testament. It tells that story in such a way that Jesus is Israel's long-awaited and promised Messiah. At the heart of the story of Jesus, however, two earth-shattering events come to the fore: his death and his resurrection. Messiahs, so it was thought, do not die; they rule. But Jesus died, and the astounding fact is that he was raised from the dead, that he ascended into heaven to sit on the throne and so become the world's true ruler.

Baptism is the *passive* act of being plunged into the story of Jesus, with those two prominent events taking front stage. We are baptized into his death and into his resurrection. We die with Jesus and we are raised with Jesus. "Gospel" then is the operative word to explain what baptism is all about: it is about being dipped into the life of Jesus. We are plunged into his life by our baptism. It is about what God has done, not what we are qualified to do.

Baptism is one of the purest moments of declaring, enacting, embodying, and understanding the gospel itself. In baptism the gospel is put into motion.

Fourth Word: Conversion

While the gospel itself is the announcement about Jesus—about who he is and what he has accomplished—there is also a proper response to that announcement. What is the proper response to the gospel? The proper and necessary response to the gospel is expressed in two terms. We let Paul define the gospel, so we can now let his fellow apostle Peter begin to define the response. The first term of response is found in the first gospel sermon Peter preached, and it occurred on another earth-shattering day, the day of Pentecost: "*Repent* and be baptized, every one of you, in the name of Jesus Christ for the forgiveness of your sins. And you will receive the gift of the Holy Spirit. The promise is for you and your children and for all who are far off—for all whom the Lord our God will call" (Acts 2:38–39).

The second term of response can be found in the aftermath of Pentecost: "But many who heard the message *believed*" (Acts 4:4). Some time later when the evangelist Philip preached, it is said, "when they *believed* Philip as he proclaimed the good news of the kingdom of God and the name of Jesus Christ, they were baptized, both men and women" (Acts 8:12).

Those two terms—"repent" and "believe"—are the proper and necessary response to the gospel itself. At baptism we declare who Jesus is, and who Jesus is determines the proper response, and the response is to surrender ourselves to him, it is to trust him, it is to turn from who we were to who he is, it is to declare our allegiance to Jesus.[11] These terms together are what we mean by the word "conversion."

Many will now ask how this can possibly apply to an infant at baptism, and the answer to that requires a brief discussion of conversion.[12] For many, conversion is a sudden act, something along the line of the experience of the apostle Paul. Sudden conversions are far more often the experience of those who were not nurtured in a Christian family. But then there's Peter. We know Paul suddenly surrendered his life even if we suspect he had experiences with Christians that were at work in his soul prior to this Damascus Road experience. But what about Peter? When was he converted? Let's look at Peter.[13] When do you date his conversion? In John 1, when Andrew informs Simon (Peter) that he has found the Messiah? Or is it in Luke 5, when Peter, after fishing all night long without trapping a single tilapia, is told by Jesus to fish on the side, which he does, and when he has hauled a mighty catch falls before Jesus and confesses his sins? Or is it in Mark 8, when Peter confesses that Jesus is the Messiah? Or is it in John 21, when after denying Jesus, Peter gets back on the journey of faith? Or is it in Acts 2, when he receives the empowerment of the Holy Spirit? Or is it in Acts 10–11, when Peter realizes finally that the gospel is for all? Here's the answer: Yes. Peter responded over and over to fresh illuminations of the gospel, and one can say for Peter—and for nearly every Christian who has ever lived (and I can't think of any exceptions)—that conversion is a lifelong process and journey of surrenderings and taking-backs and surrenderings. Furthermore, behind Peter's response to Jesus—whichever event you choose—was a life that prepared him for those responses. Peter, like Paul, was circumcised as an infant and nurtured into the covenant and law and faithfulness as an Israelite by his family and by his rabbi teachers and by his friends.

Paul shows one kind of conversion and Peter another. In the history of the church there have been three basic approaches to conversion.[14] Those approaches create and establish distinct cultures in the church, and those cultures are, to put it mildly, allergic to one another. For some, conversion is a sudden event—like Paul's and Martin Luther's and Chuck Colson's. There is a moment when a person surrenders, believes, confesses, repents, and gets baptized. Call this the personal-decision approach to conversion. For others, conversion is a sociological process that ties a person's personal, psychological, intellectual, and social development to a person's spiritual development and formation. Call this the social approach to conversion. A third approach is more liturgical or sacramental. Conversion occurs (most often) during the first two decades of a person's life as that person is baptized, catechized, and confirmed. In some traditions there is a "first Communion." Call this the liturgical approach to conversion. It is clear that the social and the liturgical approaches overlap in important ways, though the liturgical has more emphasis on sacramental moments in the church. These approaches to conversion are not only allergic to one another at times—ask someone who converted from a personal-decision approach to a Roman Catholic church or an Anglican church, or someone from the Orthodox Church who becomes either strongly Reformed or a Willow Creek–baptized convert fully devoted to Christ—but they are also shapers of how the gospel is preached and how the Christian life is understood in a local church.

There is a way to bring all three of these emphases into one church and into one culture, but it requires that a local church not only shape conversion through the liturgical events and social developments but hold firmly as well—through both of those processes—to the necessity of personal faith.

Infant baptism fits in this eclectic understanding of conversion. As the Israelites initiated their children into the faith of Israel by circumcision (for boys) and by the spiritually formative practices of rituals and instruction and prayers and synagogue attendance, so the early church "fulfilled" circumcision with infant baptism *as the first step in the journey into the Christian faith*. As circumcision without growing into heart trust and obedience does not bring circumcision to the goal of spiritual maturity, so infant baptism without growing into heart trust and obedience does not accomplish spiritual maturity. If we think of infant baptism as a "seed" of grace and faith planted in the heart of the child, then without water and sun and nurturing the seed sadly dies. The necessity of continuing response to Christ is why article 25 in the Thirty-Nine Articles of Religion says the sacraments are to be received "worthily." Thus, "in such only as *worthily receive* the same, they have a wholesome effect or operation: but they that receive them *unworthily*, purchase to themselves damnation, as Saint Paul saith."[15] Article 26 clarifies what "worthily" means: it means faith. Thus, "as by faith, and rightly, do receive the Sacraments." In article 28, with respect to the sacrament of the Lord's Supper, the terms are all brought together: "insomuch that to such as rightly, worthily, and with faith, receive the same."[16] The terms "rightly," "worthily," and "with faith" each speak to the necessity of those baptized growing into faith for the seed of redemption planted at baptism to grow into spiritual maturity and final salvation. Apart from repentance and faith, two major elements of the journey of conversion, there is no salvation. But let this be an emphasis to keep in mind: we do not by our faith make ourselves worthy of baptism. Baptism is an act of God's grace in us that we simply receive. Faith is the proper response to that grace.

Baptism, whether infant or adult, needs to be seen for what the Bible says it is: the beginning of a journey that God initiates. Wisdom prompts us to treat infant baptism as a seed planted in the heart of a child, but it is a seed in need of care, water, and sun. Conversion is a process, and it begins when the infant is baptized.

Fifth Word: Debate

There are some big debates about baptism, and sometimes you'd think by how people talk that if you get baptism wrong your salvation is in jeopardy—or at least you are close to being a heretic. Karl Barth has a word for all of us about civility when it comes to discussing baptism. This powerful Swiss theologian was nurtured into his faith through infant baptism but switched sides later in his life. Turning baptistic surely brought him into many heated debates. His response drew from experience: "An important sign that a defender of infant [or adult] baptism is certain that his cause has a sound theological basis ought surely to be . . . that he is able to present and support it calmly."[17]

Long ago I read a book called *The Water That Divides*, and on my desk as I write this paragraph is a book called *Baptism: Three Views* and another one called *Understanding Four Views on Baptism*.[18] Are there three or four? Oddly enough, the three-views book includes a view not even covered in the four-views book! The three-views book discusses believer's baptism, infant baptism, and dual baptism (performing both infant and adult-profession baptism in the same church). What are the four views? The Baptist view understands baptism as a (mere) symbol of Christ's saving work, and adult believer's baptism as only for the one who professes faith in Christ. The Reformed view is that baptism is a sacrament of the covenant; the Reformed are known for baptizing infants whose parents are believers, but they also practice adult baptism for new adult believers. The Lutheran view is that God's act in baptism is regenerative; Lutherans, too, baptize both infants and adult converts. Finally, the stronger side of the Restorationist churches view a believer's (adult's) baptism as the biblical *occasion* of salvation.[19] Four views seem enough, except that these books ignore the Eastern Orthodox and the Roman Catholic views! These two very large church bodies, each of which sees itself as the true successor to the apostles(!), perceive more redemptive work of God in the act of baptism than do the above three or four.[20] Baptism can indeed be "the water that divides." How important is that division?

One of the saddest stories in the history of the church has to do with this baptism division. In the sixteenth century some of the Anabaptists, who got their name because they were baptized "again" (or rebaptized), were thrown into a river in Zurich for what their executioners-in-the-name-of-Christ called their "third baptism." Such persons often had their hands tied and then tucked behind their knees, a pole placed between hands and legs to prevent a Houdini-like escape, and were then tossed into the water to drown because they were against infant baptism and affirmed believer's baptism. Capital punishment for believer's baptism is a disgrace to Christ and his body. Believer's baptism cost thousands of serious Christians their lives. This history is to be regretted and repudiated. All churches today that baptize infants need to take a stand on behalf of their Christian brothers and sisters who believe exclusively in adult baptism, not by agreeing with them but by supporting religious liberty and freedom of conscience. We can be grateful that today we live with such liberty, but we ought not to ignore the history of the Anabaptists who helped pave the way for such liberties by giving their lives.[21] Our baptisms today may divide us, but the division is mild compared to the days of the earliest Anabaptists. This division between us should never exceed debate and should never lead to death.

This book is written from the angle of the Anglican Communion, which is made up of Anglicans of all stripes who are involved and take sides in this debate. So where does the Anglican Communion stand in this debate about baptism? Here is the (seemingly) official position in the Anglican statement of faith, the Thirty-Nine Articles of Religion. Because the older style sentence structure makes it difficult to read, I have reformatted it and added numbers to better facilitate our discussion:

> Baptism is (1) not only a sign of profession, and mark of difference, whereby Christian [persons] are discerned from others that be not christened,
>
> (2) but it is also a sign of Regeneration or New-Birth,
>
> (3) whereby, as by an instrument, they that receive Baptism rightly are grafted into the Church;
>
> (4) the promises of the forgiveness of sin, and of our adoption to be the [children] of God by the Holy Ghost, are visibly signed and sealed; Faith is confirmed, and Grace increased by virtue of prayer unto God.[22]

Baptism, then, is (1) a "sign" and "mark of difference" that distinguishes Christians from non-Christians. It marks a difference because (2) it is a "sign" of our redemption. Those who are so baptized and so marked (3) enter into the church. Baptism leads a person into (4) various blessings. But notice the order in the journey into a baptismal faith: promised forgiveness and adoption as well as confirmation of that person's faith and the increase of grace in a person's life through an ongoing relation with God in prayer. Baptism for Anglicans thus *accomplishes* something real. (I will examine what infant baptism *does* below.) This is where we stand in this debate about baptism.

It is not likely that Baptists, Anglicans, Presbyterians, Roman Catholics, and the Orthodox are going to come to a common statement of faith on baptism any time soon. Nor am I waiting for that moment to write this book. *It Takes a Church to Baptize* is for those who are considering infant baptism in the Anglican Communion, though it will be of use to any who are considering infant baptism.

Sixth Word: Heritage

Some of the finest Christians I have known and some of my favorite theologians were baptized as infants, never got rebaptized, and teach and practice infant baptism. I date myself, but I think of John Stott and Tim Keller and J. I. Packer and Michael Green, of Martin Luther and John Calvin, of C. S. Lewis and J. R. R. Tolkien, of Dorothy Sayers and Morna Hooker and Fleming Rutledge and G. K. Chesterton and Desmond Tutu . . . and the list could grow for years and years. Of course, I know plenty of good folks on the other side too, but my point is that infant baptism is owned by lots of wonderful thinkers and leaders in the church. I recall during college being with a missions group and encountering a German Lutheran young man whose piety was extraordinary, his prayer life very deep, his grasp of the Bible far beyond mine, his passion for evangelism palpable—and then I learned he was a Lutheran who had been baptized as a child, and it got me, an unyielding Baptist, wondering how piety that rich was possible.

But this book is not about me; it's about you, your child, and our church. It's about what the Bible says about baptism and how many great thinkers in the church have understood it.

The Lutheran Dietrich Bonhoeffer, my favorite theologian, entered into a discussion about baptism with some Lutherans who, contrary to a tradition of more than four hundred years, were questioning infant baptism and advocating for baptism only upon profession of faith.[23] His opening statement in his discussion gets right to the point: "The practice of infant baptism cannot be directly proven in the New Testament." But, he continues, it "can nevertheless be seen as probable there."[24] Bonhoeffer thinks the practice of infant baptism may not be in the New Testament, but its theology is to be anchored in the Bible securely. *It Takes a Church to Baptize* will continue and expand this line of thinking.

On top of these individual theologians, we have to deal with the biggest "thinker" of all: the comprehensive witness of the church throughout the sweep of Christian history.[25] The quotations that follow are from some of the great thinkers of Christian orthodoxy in church history, people who are the creators of the Christian heritage on infant baptism.[26]

Irenaeus: "He came to save all through means of Himself—all, I say, who through him are born again to God—infants, and children, and boys and youths, and old men" (*Against Heresies* 2.22.4).

Hippolytus: "The children shall be baptized first. All of the children who can answer for themselves, let them answer. If there are any children who cannot answer for themselves, let their parents answer for them, or someone else from their family" (*Apostolic Tradition* 21.4).

Origen: "On this account also the church had a tradition from the apostles to give baptism even to infants. For they to whom the secrets of the divine mysteries were given knew that there is in all persons the natural stains of sin which must be washed away by the water and the Spirit. On account of these stains the body itself is called the 'body of sin'" (*Commentary on Romans* 5.9.11, on Rom. 6:5–6).[27]

Gregory of Nazianzus: Gregory of Nazianzus offers a mild rebuke to a mother who fears a son being baptized: "Have you an infant child? Do not let sin get any opportunity, but let him [the child] be sanctified from his childhood; from his very tenderest age let him be consecrated by the Spirit. Fearest thou the Seal [of baptism] on account of the weakness of his nature. O what a small-souled mother, and how little faith!" (*Oration on Holy Baptism* 17).

John Chrysostom: "You see how many are the benefits of baptism, and some think its heavenly grace consists only in the remission of sins, but we have enumerated ten honors [it bestows]! For this reason we baptize even infants, though they are not defiled by [personal] sins, so that there may be given to them holiness, righteousness, adoption, inheritance, brotherhood with Christ, and that they may be his [Christ's] members" (*Against Julian* 1.6.21).

Augustine: "By this grace baptized infants too are ingrafted into his [Christ's] body, infants who certainly are not yet able to imitate anyone. Christ, in whom all are made alive . . . gives also the most hidden grace of his Spirit to believers, grace which he secretly infuses even into infants. . . . It is an excellent thing that the Punic [North African] Christians call baptism salvation and the sacrament of Christ's Body nothing else than life. Whence does this derive, except from an ancient and, as I suppose, apostolic tradition, by which the churches of Christ hold inherently that without baptism and participation at the table of the Lord it is impossible for any man to attain either to the kingdom of God or to salvation and life eternal? This is the witness of Scripture, too. . . . If anyone wonders why children born of the baptized should themselves be baptized, let him attend briefly to this. . . . The sacrament of baptism is most assuredly the sacrament of regeneration" (*Forgiveness and the Just Deserts of Sin, and the Baptism of Infants* 1.9.10; 1.24.34; 2.27.43).

As in this text, Augustine thought infant baptism was apostolic: "The custom of Mother Church in baptizing infants is certainly not to be scorned, nor is it to be regarded in any way as superfluous, nor is it to be believed that its tradition is anything except apostolic" (*Literal Interpretation of Genesis* 10.23.39).

It might be important to read these quotations again with the knowledge that these theologians formed what you and I—Anglican or not—believe as Christian orthodoxy. Each was as "evangelical" in personal faith as we are, and each was as committed to the baptism of infants. This simply can't be dismissed as some kind of breach of contract with the apostles. Though the church could be wrong on this point, at least by the second century the church practiced baptism of infants. The biggest "thinker" of them all, then, is the church as a tradition, and one ought to observe that for three-quarters of the history of the church there is remarkably a *total absence of baptism for professing believers alone*. That is, for three-quarters of church history baptism was for infants.[28] Professing-faith baptism, which had its revival among the Swiss Anabaptists and then was part of a strong and respectable Baptist movement, has often been understood as a recovery of apostolic conviction. Not so fast, I will argue. For to come to that conclusion one must also believe the church simply got this wrong for a long, long time. I am prepared to draw such conclusions myself if the evidence establishes such a conviction, but I am no longer convinced the evidence must be interpreted in that manner. There is then nothing less than a powerful history of noble theologians who affirmed infant baptism.

What concerns many, however, is not the heritage of the church but the Bible, so I want to show that the church's practice developed straight from the Bible.

2

Baptism

CHURCH AND FAMILY

What distinguishes some Christians from others is what they believe, their theology, their system of thought, or their philosophy. They size one another up on the basis of their theological answers to their special theological questions. Presbyterians are connected to the theology of John Calvin, and Methodists find their guidance in John Wesley. What distinguishes each group is its theology.

What distinguishes Anglicans even more than their theology is their worship, a pattern of worship that looks back to Thomas Cranmer.[1] In fact, one of our mottos, in Latin, is *lex orandi, lex credendi*: the law of prayer is the law of belief. This is a way of saying that what unifies us is not so much a specific systematic theology but a way of worshiping that we find in *The Book of Common Prayer*. This is why our motto matters. In and through and during and because of our worship we learn the central themes of the Anglican faith and theology. It would not be uncommon for an Anglican leader to be asked, "What do you believe?" and for the leader to respond, "Come to our church for a season." In that worship event the person would hear and watch and participate in the answer. The theology of the Anglican Communion is heard, repeated, and experienced in worship based on our worship manual.

It Takes a Church to Baptize, therefore, will be structured by the liturgy for Holy Baptism in *The Book of Common Prayer*.[2] You will learn what we believe by entering into how we worship.

The Opening of the Service for Baptism

On a Sunday when a baptism occurs in our church there is a buzz in the air. New people we've not seen before arrive, the pastors and parents are covering last-second details, and the sanctuary is often full. A baptism is a big event in the Anglican Church, as it witnesses to God's grace of new life in Christ, the purification of the water, the welcoming of a new child into our church, and the participation of the family and the whole church in a public commitment to support this child in the faith. In baptism we welcome a child into the family of faith. If an adult is being baptized, we welcome the adult.

When everyone has entered into the sanctuary, we begin with these words (or similar words of greeting) from our priest, Father Jay Greener:

Celebrant: Alleluia. Christ is risen.

People: The Lord is risen indeed. Alleluia.

I did not grow up Anglican, so every time we do this call and response I get charged by both the appropriateness of the words and the participation of the audience. Our faith is rooted in the resurrection of Christ, so the announcement that Christ is risen prompts us to shout "Alleluia!" What better response could there be? (During Lent we do not utter the word "alleluia" in our worship.)

I have used words such as "our" and "church" and "family" in our discussion thus far to emphasize that baptism is not just about one person and her God but about a person surrounded by her family and the church in the context of God's grace. We prepare ourselves for the baptism as our pastor begins with words that make a church context for baptism abundantly clear:[3]

Celebrant: There is one Body and one Spirit;
    People: There is one hope in God's call to us;
Celebrant: One Lord, one Faith, one Baptism;
    People: One God and Father of all.
Celebrant: The Lord be with you.
    People: And also with you.
Celebrant: Let us pray.

This is the best, as well as the one and only, place to begin a baptismal service. The church is gathered together as one body in the power of the one Spirit as we celebrate our one hope, Lord, faith, baptism, and the one God and Father.

Some might ask, Why not just baptize someone in the river or in my home all alone? The answer is already given: because baptisms are church events in which the church surrounds a family's decision to bring their infant into the fellowship of the church. Or they are church events in which an adult is being baptized surrounded by family and the church, or only by the church fellowship. In all cases, baptisms are church events. At times in the history of the church baptisms unfortunately have become little more than "me and God"—that is, some people don't think they need a surrounding church family for baptism. There is a website for everything, including one for self-baptism! But this is not the way of the church. Baptisms historically have been public, they have been in the context of a minister of the gospel, and they have occurred in the context of the fellowship of other Christians and families. Baptism is a church event.[4]

The introductory words are followed by praying together a formal prayer, a collect, determined by the day in the church calendar. Then we read Scripture aloud—a lesson from the Old Testament, a prayer from the Psalms, and another lesson from a New Testament letter, and finally we all stand as a deacon reads the Gospel lesson for the day. After the readings someone gives a sermon. This reading of Scripture followed by a sermon is typical of an Anglican worship service. However, there is something special about this day and this event. The baptismal service is special because it is a family event: it is special because everyone can see the family of those who are about to be baptized sitting up front awaiting the event. Moms and dads and grandpas and grandmas and family and friends do their best to pay attention, but distraction in such a case is as common as the event is sacred.

The Family-Church Context for Infant Baptism

That we baptize infants may surprise and even annoy and trouble some readers, especially those raised in baptistic churches where one must make a profession of faith prior to baptism. In bringing our infants to church for baptism we are following in the path God established for Israel long, long ago when God first established a covenant with our father, Abraham. Two major events occurred: first, God made a promise and entered into a legal obligation to be faithful to that promise by passing between the sacrificed animals Abraham laid out on the ground, and second, God told Abraham to get circumcised (Gen. 15; 17). To show how important circumcision was to covenant, God said this to Abraham:

> This is my covenant with you and your descendants after you, the covenant you are to keep: Every male among you shall be circumcised. You are to undergo circumcision, and it will be the sign of the covenant between me and you. For the generations to come every male among you who is eight days old must be circumcised, including those born in your household or bought with money from a foreigner—those who are not your offspring. Whether born in your household or bought with your money, they must be circumcised. My covenant in your flesh is to be an everlasting covenant. Any uncircumcised male, who has not been circumcised in the flesh, will be cut off from his people; he has broken my covenant. (Gen. 17:10–14)

Circumcision in the Bible was both the covenant and the sign of the covenant. The snipping off of the foreskin was the entry rite, the act that turned a child into a covenant-family member. Abraham's son Isaac did not choose to become a member of Abraham's family; Abraham and Sarah made that choice. More accurately, of course, God made that choice, just as God made the choice to bring Abraham into God's covenant family. God did it all. Abraham only affirmed, believed, and surrendered himself to God's covenant. As a part of his surrender Abraham underwent the ritual of circumcision.

Why then did God also tell Abraham and all his covenant descendants to circumcise their baby boys on the eighth day? Because covenant formation was a family affair. Abraham's faith meant he would usher his own children into the faith through the covenant rite of circumcision, through example and instruction and ritual. It is best then to say that circumcision both made the child a member of the covenant people and launched him into a journey with the covenant people.

At the core of a church is the family, so baptism as a church event is just as much a family event. The core group in a church is not the church staff or the sanctuary or the Sunday school classrooms but the family. This pertains as much to a single person, who forms a family of one, as to a nuclear family where one family is integrated generationally. At Church of the Redeemer we have some single folks, and we have a few families that are multigenerational, including Kris's and mine. Quickly think through the Bible's entire story and you will see at its core the family: Abraham and Sarah and children; Moses, a family man who instructed Israel through its family leaders and the laws that take family into consideration all the time; the families who celebrated the central feasts of Israel; David and his wives and his many children, who expanded family beyond God's designs but were nonetheless a family; Isaiah and his wife and his sons with odd names; and finally, Joseph, Mary, and Jesus, along with Jesus's brothers and sisters, who were the "holy family." Jesus may well have challenged various family members to put him first, but he did not denigrate the family as the family. On the cross he made sure his mother was cared for by John. Then think of how Paul chose to instruct the churches of Ephesus and Colossae. What did he do? He instructed them by informing fathers and mothers and children how now to conduct themselves as Christians in the Roman Empire.

Many skilled historians have shown again and again that it was the forces of modernity and the Enlightenment in the seventeenth and eighteenth centuries and beyond that led to the decentralization of the family and its replacement with the individual ego as the center of society. Add to this that sociologists have pointed to a deep pathology in our country because individualism has replaced family and social obligations.[5] God's way from the very beginning was the family, and that means God's design is to reach the individual through the family and not the family through the individual. Nothing has been more harmful to covenant-shaped discipleship in the Western church than decentralizing the family and replacing it with the individual ego. Church leader after church leader has called us to reconsider the importance of family and the integration of children into worship.[6] The biggest challenge to infant baptism today comes not from the Bible so much as from rampant individualism.

Because families are central to the covenant formation of our children, we baptize infants. In this belief we are not hopeless romantics lost in the mists of colonial America nostalgia. Rather, we have inherited an ancient plan. Family-centered faith formation was the plan of God from the very beginning: a parent, when entering into the covenant, brought all the children into that covenant relation. Religion wasn't a choice; it was a family inheritance in the ancient Near East and in the Middle East in the first century with Jesus (who was circumcised), with Paul (who was too), and with all the early Christians.

Three conclusions now: first, God created and established the covenant with Abraham and his family, and it was not at all Abraham's idea; second, covenant participation is a family affair from the beginning; third, a father's covenant relation with God entailed covenant participation of that father's entire family (one can say the same about mothers). The faith of Abraham, one could say, counted for Isaac's faith as he grew into (or out of) that covenant faith. I could add another point to say the "family" becomes a "nation" in the Old Testament, and that nation becomes a "church" in the New Testament. So we are back to where we began: baptism is an act of God that occurs in the context of a family and a church.

Infant baptism, I have heard more than one time, is like being made a citizen of the United States because US-born citizens have what is called "birthright citizenship."[7] We are automatically included in membership in the country and are immediately granted the rights and duties pertaining to citizenship. The child doesn't make that choice. The Fourteenth Amendment puts it this way: "All persons born or naturalized in the United States, and subject to the jurisdiction thereof, are citizens of the United States and of the State wherein they reside." Only over time does one grow into citizenship and learn how to be a good citizen, but the fact of one's citizenship was established at birth by an act of Congress. So with infant baptism: it is granted by God's grace to those who are born into a Christian family to be baptized into the church family, and only over time does the baptized child grow into mature adulthood in faith. Once again, we emphasize that conversion in the Bible is a journey into spiritual maturity, and it begins at baptism. Baptism is an act of God's grace, not something we do to someone.

Baptisms and Imitation

Children who grow up watching infant baptisms and who participate in those sacred events somehow develop, as Marilynne Robinson tells so wondrously in her fictional stories about Pastor John Ames, an instinct for baptism. It may be questions about what and why, or it may be baptizing bath toys and dolls, or it may involve the baptism of cats—yes, even cats! Through the words of Pastor Ames we are secreted into a wonderful little story from his childhood:

Now, this might seem a trivial thing to mention, considering the gravity of the subject, but I truly don't feel it is. We were very pious children from pious households in a fairly pious town, and this affected our behavior considerably. Once, we baptized a litter of cats. They were dusty little barn cats just steady on their legs, the kind of waifish creatures that live their anonymous lives keeping the mice down and have no interest in humans at all, except to avoid them. But the animals all seem to start out sociable, so we were always pleased to find new kittens prowling out of whatever cranny their mother had tried to hide them in, as ready to play as we were. It occurred to one of the girls to swaddle them up in a doll's dress—there was only one dress, which was just as well since the cats could hardly tolerate a moment in it and would have to have been unswaddled as soon as they were christened in any case. I myself moistened their brows, repeating the full Trinitarian formula.[8]

Baptizing kittens is not seen by all as a good Christian thing to do, so they heard from the kittens' mother, who carried them away, some still unbaptized. But that only gave the children an opportunity to ask their pastor and father, John Ames, about baptism. There is more, as I have said, caught than taught, but what is caught has been taught. They were taught that baptism was a sacred act and not for kittens, but they had caught more than that.

Their grim old crooked-tailed mother found us baptizing away by the creek and began carrying her babies off by the napes of their necks, one and then another. We lost track of which was which, but we were fairly sure that some of the creatures had been borne away still in the darkness of paganism, and that worried us a good deal. So finally I asked my father in the most offhand way imaginable what exactly would happen to a cat if one were to, say, baptize it. He replied that the Sacraments must always be treated and regarded with the greatest respect. That wasn't really an answer to my question. We did respect the Sacraments, but we thought the whole world of those cats. I got his meaning, though, and I did no more baptizing until I was ordained.

What I enjoyed most about this wonderful story by Robinson comes next, which leads right back to the classic debate between those who do and those who don't baptize infants.

Two or three of that litter were taken home by the girls and made into fairly respectable house cats. Louisa took a yellow one. She still had it when we were married. The others lived out their feral lives, indistinguishable from their kind, whether pagan or Christian no one could ever tell. She called her cat Sparkle, for the white patch on its forehead. It disappeared finally. I suspect it got caught stealing rabbits, a sin to which it was much given, Christian cat that we knew it to be, stiff-jointed as it was by that time. One of the boys said she should have named it Sprinkle. He was a Baptist, a firm believer in total immersion, which those cats should have been grateful I was not. He told us no effect at all could be achieved by our methods, and we could not prove him wrong. Our Soapy must be a distant relative.

This dear old pastor echoes now a kind of theology made well known by Saint Francis of Assisi, one dipped deeply in the importance of ritual and the power of God at work in baptisms.

I still remember how those warm little brows felt under the palm of my hand. Everyone has petted a cat, but to touch one like that, with the pure intention of blessing it, is a very different thing. It stays in the mind. For years we would wonder what, from a cosmic viewpoint, we had done to them. It still seems to me to be a real question. There is a reality in blessing, which I take baptism to be, primarily. It doesn't enhance sacredness, but it acknowledges it, and there is a power in that. I have felt it pass through me, so to speak. The sensation is of really knowing a creature, I mean really feeling its mysterious life and your own mysterious life at the same time. I don't wish to be urging the ministry on you, but there are some advantages to it you might not know to take account of if I did not point them out. Not that you have to be a minister to confer blessing. You are simply much more likely to find yourself in that position. It's a thing people expect of you. I don't know why there is so little about this aspect of the calling in the literature.

This story puts into print a very common habit children have of doing what they see being done—a sacred habit, I would say, of making what is not sacred something sacred. The baptismal service, like so many acts in a church, becomes an opportunity for children to observe and then go imitate. Imitation is central to spiritual formation, and we infant baptizers are not alone in having our children imitate us. Baptists do much the same thing.

Harper Lee penned such a story of baptism by Baptist-types in her novel *Go Set a Watchman*. Lee tells the story of the children in the novel, reeling under the impact of a local revivalist's preaching of hellfire and damnation and then going forward and repenting and getting baptized, who recreate and imitate a revival service:

> Jem preached the longest, most tedious sermon she ever heard in her life. He said that sin was about the most sinful thing he could think of, and no one who sinned could be a success, and blessed was he who sat in the seat of the scornful; in short, he repeated his own version of everything they had heard for the past three nights. . . .
> He started on hell, but she said, "Now cut it out, Jem."
> Reverend Moorehead's description of it was enough to last

her a lifetime. Jem reversed his field and tackled heaven: heaven was full of bananas (Dill's love) and scalloped potatoes (her favorite), and when they died they would go there and eat good things until Judgement Day, but on Judgement Day, God, having written down everything they did in a book from the day they were born, would cast them into hell.

Jem drew the service to a close by asking all who wished to be united with Christ to step forward. She went.

Jem put his hand on her head and said, "Young lady, do you repent?"

"Yes sir," she said.

"Have you been baptized?"

"No sir," she said.

"Well—" Jem dipped his hand into the black water of the fishpool and laid it on her head. "I baptize you—"

"Hey, wait a minute!" shouted Dill. "That's not right!"

"I reckon it is," said Jem. "Scout and me are Methodists."

"Yeah, but we're having a Baptist revival. You've got to duck her. I think I'll be baptized, too." The ramifications of the ceremony were dawning on Dill, and he fought hard for the role. "I'm the one," he insisted. "I'm the Baptist so I reckon I'm the one to be baptized." . . .

Jem took her by the hand and guided her into the pool. The water was warm and slimy, and the bottom was slippery. "Don't you duck me but once," she said.

Jem stood on the edge of the pool. The figure beneath the sheet joined him and flapped its arms wildly. Jem held her back and pushed her under. As her head went beneath the surface she heard Jem intoning, "Jean Louise Finch, I baptize you in the name of—"[9]

This hilarious story is interrupted not by a mother cat but by a disciplinarian who seemingly can't play along with the sacred imitation of children. But enough has been told to make the point: children do what they've seen done, including sacred actions such as baptism. The children of *Gilead* and the children of *Go Set a Watchman* learned baptism by participating in baptism services themselves. They illustrate the heart of Anglican worship: we learn our theology in our worship (even if both sets of children in these two stories will need to grow into a better theology of baptism).

Resistance and Personal Faith

Some still resist the idea of baptizing infants because they want to throw primary emphasis on the personal faith of the individual believer. No one wants to discount personal, individual faith, nor should one say that the infant who is baptized has his or her redemption all taken care of in spite of being completely unaware. No, the pattern of the Bible is divinely originated, family-based covenant formation: the father (or mother in some situations) is brought into the covenant and brings the rest of the family along, and part of that bringing along is rearing and nurturing the child into the covenant faith so that the child grows into a responsible, adult covenant member. The infant's baptism launches that child on a journey into spiritual maturity. This has to be emphasized because it can too easily be ignored by so many who don't read the Old Testament often enough: God designed with Abraham a pattern in which the parent's faith implicates the child in that faith. From the beginning of our covenant faith, the child was brought into the faith on the basis of the parent's faith.

This is why we baptize infants, though there are other reasons, and we will bring those into the discussion as we proceed through the liturgy for the baptism.

3

Presentation and Commitments

After the Scripture reading and sermon, everything in the service turns toward the baptism. Our pastor presents the candidates for baptism to the whole church family. If an adult happens to be being baptized, that person will speak for herself or himself. Also, in accordance with a very old church tradition, candidates for baptism have "sponsors," Christians in our church who can reliably testify that this candidate is a Christian and worthy of baptism.[1] Our pastor then asks a question of each person presented:

Celebrant: Do you desire to be baptized?
Candidate: I do.

If the candidate is an infant, he is presented by parents or godparents who say, "I present Theo to receive the sacrament of baptism."

The service for baptism now turns a corner into some very serious questions for everyone present, those who are privileged to participate in the essence of baptism as a church event. This turning to the church as the context for baptism embodies our covenant-family-based understanding of baptism and illustrates it to those who have never witnessed anything like it.

Three Levels of Commitment

Our pastor now asks for a significant commitment on the part of the parents and godparents of the infants. Anglican theologian J. I. Packer helpfully speaks here of "two-way covenanting"—that is, God covenants with us to redeem, and we covenant with God to nurture someone in the faith.[2] What is done in the baptism service lines up perfectly with Israel's famous Shema from Deuteronomy 6, which draws us once again into the depths of the Bible's pattern of covenant as family-, nation-, and church-based spiritual formation:

> Hear, O Israel: The LORD our God, the LORD is one. Love the LORD your God with all your heart and with all your soul and with all your strength. These commandments that I give you today are to be on your hearts. *Impress them on your children. Talk about them when you sit at home and when you walk along the road, when you lie down and when you get up.* Tie them as symbols on your hands and bind them on your foreheads. Write them on the doorframes of your houses and on your gates. (vv. 4–9)[3]

If it were not for the customary nature of these historic words in the Bible or even the words that are being read from the baptismal liturgy, their content might stun us with the seriousness of what is being said. This is nothing less than a public commitment on the part of parents and godparents, in response to God's grace, to be responsible for the spiritual formation of these children and to nurture them into the faith. *The first level of this commitment, then, is to raise our family in the faith. Common Worship* puts it this way:

Celebrant: Faith is the gift of God to his people. In baptism the Lord is adding to our number those whom he is calling. People of God, will you welcome these children/candidates and uphold them in their new life in Christ?

All: With the help of God, we will.

The words that follow are common to or similar in all presentations for Holy Baptism. They emphasize the commitment of the family to nurture the child into the faith:

Celebrant: Will you be responsible for seeing that the child you present is brought up in the Christian faith and life?

Parents and Godparents: I will, with God's help.

Celebrant: Will you by your prayers and witness help this child to grow into the full stature of Christ?

Parents and Godparents: I will, with God's help.

Perhaps we need to spend more time in our church classes or home Bible studies or in our sermons drawing more attention to the seriousness of our church family's public commitment. What is clear is that the parents and godparents assume in these words a serious responsibility to nurture children in the faith.

Kara Powell and Chap Clark's splendid book *Sticky Faith* reminds us that parents get in their children what they (the parents)

themselves are.[4] Their contention also is that the splendid education model of one teacher for every five students in a small group
needs to be reversed to create "sticky faith." That is, it takes at
least five adult mentors to establish sticky faith in the life of one
young person. Unfortunately, their studies have revealed only
one out of eight youth talk about the Christian faith with their
Christian mothers, while only one out of twenty do with their
Christian fathers! This sad approach far too often creates a very
slippery faith. Anglican Michael Green, speaking as one who is
both experienced with many baptisms and exasperated by the
inattentiveness and lack of seriousness shown by church leaders, churches, parents, and sponsors when it comes to nurturing
the faith of the baptized, sets forth nothing less than a warning:

> [Baptism of infants] is administered with a token sprinkling
> of water, without instruction of the parents and godparents,
> without preaching, and in the middle of the afternoon when
> nobody else is there. "We want it nice and private, Vicar!"
> Alas, all of that is true in some places at some times. It is
> totally indefensible. The mark of entry into the covenant should
> be a time of celebration, of public welcome into Christ's body,
> the church. It should take place after careful instruction of the
> parents and godparents beforehand, and of the congregation at
> the occasion itself. Many of the main-line churches have been
> appallingly lax over this, and have only themselves to blame for
> the nominalism and superstition which have come to surround
> this sacrament in the minds of many.
> Baptism should take place in the body of the congregation
> at one of the main services. . . . It is not, and it cannot be right
> to make it, a hole-in-the-corner affair.[5]

Indeed. Infant baptism apart from family and church nurture is
a magical superstition that does more damage than good. The

solution to laxity by parents, sponsors, and churches, however, is not adult baptism but renewal in the hearts of parents and churches.

The first commitment in the baptismal service is for parents and godparents. *The second commitment follows as our pastor looks at the parents, the godparents, and the adults being baptized and asks for a public commitment of conversion.* But before we get to the exact words, we may need to be warned that this commitment can be jarring for many. We live in a most comfortable way with our world, so much so that the distinction—of the world from the church, or the world from the kingdom, or the world from the Christian life—for some is unintelligible. The Bible's understanding of the world is that it is unredeemed rebellion against God and is shaped by pride and power and pleasure and profit. Jesus and the apostles summoned kingdom people to turn away from the world and the kingdom of darkness—away from pride, power, pleasure, and profit—and toward the kingdom of light. Behind the world and under the world and pervading the world are Satan and his minions of evil and injustice and hatred. So from the earliest periods of the church, those being baptized—or the sponsors, parents, and godparents—were asked to commit themselves in public to turn from the world and Satan and toward God. Our pastor asks:

Question: Do you renounce Satan and all the spiritual forces of wickedness that rebel against God?

Answer: I renounce them.

Question: Do you renounce the evil powers of this world which corrupt and destroy the creatures of God?

Answer: I renounce them.

Question: Do you renounce all sinful desires that draw you from the love of God?*

Answer: I renounce them.

Question: Do you turn to Jesus Christ and accept him as your Savior?†

Answer: I do.

Question: Do you put your whole trust in his grace and love?

Answer: I do.

Question: Do you promise to follow and obey him as your Lord?

Answer: I do.

You may wonder whether this is too much, or you may be turned off by this emphasis on Satan and the evil powers of this world, but there is little we hear in our churches today that is any more resonant with the New Testament's understanding of the spiritual and cosmic battle at work in the world. In this baptismal commitment, both for sponsors and for those being baptized, we get a beautiful theology of the conflict at work in genuine conversion. To convert is to turn from the world and Satan and systemic evil and the flesh toward Christ, toward the Spirit, and toward obedience to Christ. Behind these words is the cosmic battle of the flesh and the principalities and powers against God—Father, Son, and Spirit—and God's people. As Paul puts it, "For the flesh desires what is contrary to the Spirit, and the Spirit what is contrary to the flesh. They are in conflict with each other, so that you are not to do whatever you want" (Gal. 5:17). In another letter he frames this more cosmically: "For our struggle is not against flesh and blood, but against the

---

* *Common Worship*: "from God and neighbour."

† *Common Worship* adds: "Do you submit to Christ as Lord?" The response is "I submit to Christ."

rulers, against the authorities, against the powers of this dark world and against the spiritual forces of evil in the heavenly realms" (Eph. 6:12; see whole passage at 6:10–17).

The third commitment is to the creed, the historic faith of the church.[6] The creed, too, emphasizes our church-i-ness. The creed we affirm in public is not a faith statement drawn up by one of our deacons or priests or something that our vestry voted on, nor is it a theological creed formed by the smartest theologians of our day. We confess the seventeen- or eighteen-hundred-year-old Apostles' Creed, or the Nicene Creed, as the faith of the whole church for all time.[7] Baptism and the formation of the creed were intertwined in the earliest churches, so it is both fitting and historic for us to confess our faith at a baptism. Our pastor leads us into a public call and response in the Apostles' Creed:

Celebrant: Do you believe in God the Father?

People: I believe in God, the Father almighty, creator of heaven and earth.

Celebrant: Do you believe in Jesus Christ, the Son of God?

People: I believe in Jesus Christ, his only Son, our Lord,
He was conceived by the power of the Holy Spirit
and born of the Virgin Mary.
He suffered under Pontius Pilate,
was crucified, died, and was buried.
He descended to the dead.
On the third day he rose again.
He ascended into heaven,
and is seated at the right hand of the Father.
He will come again to judge the living and the dead.

Celebrant: Do you believe in God the Holy Spirit?

People: I believe in the Holy Spirit,
the holy catholic Church,
the communion of saints,
the forgiveness of sins,
the resurrection of the body,
and the life everlasting.

Notice both how emphatic our creed is on what God has done and how totally absent is anything about what we can do or have done. Our creed reminds us in each line that baptism is something God does.

We are not yet done, because it is the pastor's responsibility to ask (yet again) for more public, responsive commitment to following Christ in fellowship, repentance, evangelism, love, and justice:[8]

Celebrant: Will you continue in the apostles' teaching and fellowship, in the breaking of the bread, and in the prayers?

People: I will, with God's help.

Celebrant: Will you persevere in resisting evil, and, whenever you fall into sin, repent and return to the Lord?

People: I will, with God's help.

Celebrant: Will you proclaim by word and example the Good News of God in Christ?

People: I will, with God's help.

Celebrant: Will you seek and serve Christ in all persons, loving your neighbor as yourself?

People: I will, with God's help.

Celebrant: Will you strive for justice and peace among all people, and respect the dignity of every human being?

People: I will, with God's help.

Some may well be taken by surprise by how penetrating and demanding, if not invasive, these commitments are. Some will think the service is getting a bit too long. The proper and historic response is that anyone who cares about the church will agree that it is commitments such as these that will establish sustainable churches that can nurture converts and infants into the faith. Such churches foster sticky faith. Of course we know that infant baptism leading into mature Christian discipleship is not a sure process. We also admit that many of us utter things aloud that we do not mean and may not carry through on, so we ask everyone in the room to pray to God for those who are being baptized that God's grace will create a stable faith. Again, this emphasizes baptism as something God is doing in our midst.

Perhaps now is a good time to mention that in the baptismal liturgy, candidates for confirmation are included with those who are being baptized. In confirmation, the genius of the family- and church-based formation comes into full view even more. After infant baptism the child is to be nurtured by family and church into the faith and catechized into the essentials of the faith. And then, usually during the early teenage years, that baptized person is presented as a confirmand. That is, the child is now deemed to have been taught and more completely accepted the faith personally. This means the baptismal service is not just for infants but for those who have personally been instructed to affirm the faith in public. It should be emphasized that it is at baptism, not confirmation, that a person is admitted into church membership.

Back to the baptismal service: A leader from the church steps forward to lead us in a series of prayer requests, but these are the prayers an entire church needs to pray on a constant basis for the children and new converts. Those in our congregation are alert to the baptisms that are taking place, and as they hear these prayers they are given the opportunity to recommit themselves to their own baptism. I know this is what happens to me each time I participate in a baptism at Church of the Redeemer, and I'm confident many others go through the same. To make this a matter of prayer is to turn our hearts to the true source of conversion and discipleship, God the Father, Son, and Holy Spirit.

We ask God to protect from sin those being baptized, to open their hearts to grace, to grant them the fresh gifts of the Spirit, to sustain them in the faith, to fill them with love, to make them instruments of the gospel in the world, and to allow them to mature into Christlikeness. Once again, notice that this baptismal service presents the Christian life as a conversion process from infant baptism through adulthood, and it does not guarantee that those baptized will become mature disciples of Jesus. So we turn to God in prayer, asking:

> Leader: Deliver them, O Lord, from the way of sin and death.
>
> People: Lord, hear our prayer.
>
> Leader: Open their hearts to your grace and truth.
>
> People: Lord, hear our prayer.
>
> Leader: Fill them with your holy and life-giving Spirit.
>
> People: Lord, hear our prayer.
>
> Leader: Keep them in the faith and communion of your holy Church.
>
> People: Lord, hear our prayer.
>
> Leader: Teach them to love others in the power of the Spirit.
>
> People: Lord, hear our prayer.
>
> Leader: Send them into the world in witness to your love.
>
> People: Lord, hear our prayer.

Leader: Bring them to the fullness of your peace and glory.

People: Lord, hear our prayer.

Then our pastor steps forward to offer his or her prayer for those who are being baptized. It is a prayer full of wisdom that I have come to appreciate deeply because of its emphasis on the gospel itself:

Grant, O Lord, that all who are baptized into the death of Jesus Christ your Son may live in the power of his resurrection and look for him to come again in glory; who lives and reigns now and forever. Amen.

This prayer reveals the heart of baptismal theology: to be baptized is to be plunged into the death of Jesus and to be raised in the resurrection of Jesus, just as it is to assume, through discipleship, a life of self-denial and victory in the Spirit.

A Wise Reminder

Not even the most gifted thinkers know what they are getting into when baptized as adults. Alexander Schmemann, the great Russian Orthodox theologian, draws our attention to the fact that we *don't understand* the gospel of Jesus's death and resurrection at our baptism; it will take a lifetime to understand it and all eternity to grasp it more completely. He helpfully reminds us that we are not saved by our knowledge and that our baptism is not dependent on our grasp of the mysteries of our faith. Likewise, baptism is not the result of passing a test of theology.[9] In fact, more than one theologian has said baptism reduces all those being baptized, whether adults or infants, to being infants. The emphasis in infant baptism now comes into view: it is not what we do that makes us worthy of baptism but what has been done for us. The work of Christ in which the infant is baptized is what brings redemption.

We need to pause here—just before the pastor baptizes those who are being presented—to think a little more about what baptism is. The next two chapters, then, are a digression into the theology of baptism and a defense of infant baptism.

4

The Three Great Themes of Our Baptism

The insight of that great Russian Orthodox Alexander Schmemann just mentioned, no matter how respected among theologians, is not the Bible. As a Bible professor, I believe our theology and our practice ought to be established by the Bible and not simply by appealing to our favorite theologians or pastors, however greatly we respect them. This has been a feature of the heart of the Anglican Communion from the outset and was formed into the sixth article in the Thirty-Nine Articles of Religion. Very few statements express the importance of Scripture for shaping what we believe as well as this article:

> Holy Scripture containeth all things necessary to salvation: so that whatsoever is not read therein, nor may be proved thereby, is not to be required of any man, that it should be believed as an article of the Faith, or be thought requisite or necessary to salvation.[1]

We learn here two fundamentals for establishing what we are to believe: First, the Bible has what we need for our redemption. Second, anything that is not in the Bible or capable of proof from the Bible is not necessary for salvation.[2] I believe in *prima scriptura*, turning first to the Bible.

To appreciate the importance of infant baptism we need to look at the meaning of baptism itself. What is baptism? What's it all about? Because we want to base our answers on the Bible, our question for this chapter is, What does the Bible say about the *meaning* of baptism? Three themes emerge about the meaning of baptism from baptism texts in the New Testament. Those three themes impact the meaning of infant baptism. In this chapter I will explain the themes, and in chapter 5 I will offer the reasons for baptizing infants.

The three themes of our baptism are (1) union with Christ, (2) Spirit and church reception, and (3) forgiveness and redemption. Each of these themes emphasizes what God has done because God loves us.

Baptism Leads to Our Union with Christ

One of the earliest reflections on the meaning of baptism can be found in a statement made by the apostle Paul when someone was baptized: "If you declare with your mouth, 'Jesus is Lord,' and believe in your heart that God raised him from the dead, you will be saved. For it is with your heart that you believe and are justified, and it is with your mouth that you profess your faith and are saved" (Rom. 10:9–10). Most experts in New Testament studies think the apostle Paul is actually quoting an early Christian creed or confession that was said at one's baptism, and they are most likely correct. No one was baptized without confessing their allegiance to Jesus as Redeemer and Lord. Even if the scholars aren't accurate about the precise origins of this set of lines now found in Romans, they are right about the importance of a confession being required at baptism. This kind of confession grew over time, as we saw in our discussion of the baptism service, into the Apostles' Creed and the Nicene Creed. Church historians have shown that creeds formed the basis for instructing new converts and were required as confessions when those converts were baptized.

That confession from the words of the apostle Paul shows that the faith of the one being baptized is *focused on Christ* and on what God has accomplished in Christ. Our first theme, then, is that baptism throughout the New Testament is about being *united with Christ* in three senses: with (1) the person of Jesus himself and therefore with (2) his death and (3) his resurrection. To be baptized is to be incorporated into Christ, the one who died and was raised.

In reading the Bible verses below, I ask you not to skip over them but to read each carefully, because on them we can build our understanding of what baptism is. The first one emphasizes union—that is, "in the name of"—not only with Christ but also with the Father and the Spirit:

> Therefore go and make disciples of all nations, baptizing them *in the name of* the Father and of the Son and of the Holy Spirit. (Matt. 28:19)

Notice how the next four verses, all from the book of Acts, understand baptism as being in the name of Jesus:

> Peter replied, "Repent and be baptized, every one of you, *in the name of* Jesus Christ for the forgiveness of your sins. And you will receive the gift of the Holy Spirit." (2:38)

. . . because the Holy Spirit had not yet come on any of them; they had simply been baptized *in the name of* the Lord Jesus. (8:16)

So he ordered that they be baptized *in the name of* Jesus Christ. Then they asked Peter to stay with them for a few days. (10:48)

On hearing this, they were baptized *in the name of* the Lord Jesus. (19:5)

To be baptized "in the name of" someone is to bring yourself into relation and into union with that person, and it implies being brought under that person's lordship. This first set of Bible verses shows then that baptism is an act that brings us into union with God—Father, Son, and Spirit. Or better yet, it is the act in which God draws us into union with Father, Son, and Spirit. (The book of Acts and the letters of Paul emphasize baptism as baptism into the name of Jesus Christ, so the trinitarian formula of Matthew 28—Father, Son, Spirit—is something the church eventually saw as expressing the fullness of baptism.)

Two other passages about baptism in the New Testament teach even more about our union with God in Christ: Romans 6:1–14 and Colossians 2:9–15. In Romans 6 Paul is aware that some Christians claim their experience of God's abundant grace means they can live in sin since forgiveness is automatic and abundant. How does Paul respond? He appeals to their baptism, plunging them right back into the waters of baptism in order to lead them out of that water into a "new life." That is, their baptism in water means and requires that they no longer live a life of sin but a life that is transformed into holiness and love. Here are Paul's words:

Or don't you know that all of us who were baptized into Christ Jesus were baptized into his death? We were therefore buried with him through baptism into death in order that, just as Christ was raised from the dead through the glory of the Father, we too may live a new life. (Rom. 6:3–4)

He goes further into a theology of baptism in the words that follow, showing that baptism is a union with the death of Christ to sin:

For we know that our old self was crucified with him so that the body ruled by sin might be done away with, that we should no longer be slaves to sin—because anyone who has died has been set free from sin. (Rom. 6:6–7)

As Christ died and slayed death itself, so Christians are to "count yourselves dead to sin but alive to God in Christ Jesus" (Rom. 6:11). Because of this baptism, the grace of God has been set loose in the life of the baptized. Paul now offers to them nothing less than a depiction of the Christian life as a baptismal life:

Do not offer any part of yourself to sin as an instrument of wickedness, but rather offer yourselves to God as those who have been brought from death to life; and offer every part of yourself to him as an instrument of righteousness. For sin shall no longer be your master, because you are not under the law, but under grace. (Rom. 6:13–14)

Baptism is union with Christ, and since Christ is the one who died and who was raised, union with Christ means dying with Christ and rising with Christ.

Now to the second special passage, Colossians 2, where Paul is facing an entirely different and seemingly (to us) bizarre problem. The Colossians have become attracted to a philosophy that diminishes the importance of Christ and exalts the "powers" or evil spirits inhabiting the world and its system, and they are being taught that the way to victory over their sinful flesh is by rigorous fasting, which will, if done well, precipitate ecstatic visions that will give them spiritual victory.[3] They were more than a little proud of their spirituality to boot. Yes, it was that complex and confused.

What was Paul's response? Their baptism.

In Colossians Paul very importantly connects baptism to circumcision. I will discuss this much more completely in chapter 5, but for now we need to see that their baptism was a union with Christ. In their baptism they died with Christ and were raised with Christ. In identifying with Jesus in his death, they identified with the one who on the cross forgave sins, canceled our debt, and disarmed the powers. Thus, they have died to those powers, the cross is the instrument of victory, and rigorous fasting and ecstatic visions are not needed for victory—all they need is to learn to indwell by faith their baptism. To use a common quip of our day: all they ever learned about the Christian life they learned in their baptism. That is my summary of Paul's teaching in Colossians 2 on the baptismal life, but here are his words, which are some of the most complicated and wondrous words ever written (the baptismal words and its blessings are in italics):

> In him you were also circumcised with a circumcision not performed by human hands. Your whole self ruled by the flesh was put off when you were circumcised by Christ, *having been buried with him in baptism, in which you were also raised with*

him through your faith in the working of God, who raised him from the dead.

When you were dead in your sins and in the uncircumcision of your flesh, God made you alive with Christ. He forgave us all our sins, having canceled the charge of our legal indebtedness, which stood against us and condemned us; he has taken it away, nailing it to the cross. And having disarmed the powers and authorities, he made a public spectacle of them, triumphing over them by the cross. (Col. 2:11–15)

At Colossae this is what matters most: the victory over the powers has already been won (at the cross and in their baptism into that cross), and they need only to indwell that victory by reminding themselves of what their baptism accomplished when they rose with the resurrected Jesus! Forget the fasting, forget the ecstatic vision, Paul is saying to them, we've got it all in Christ and have been plunged into all he has accomplished. In their baptism, as Paul says in both Romans 6 and Colossians 2, they really did die to death and its evil; in baptism they really did rise to new life in Christ.

Baptism is an act in which God brings us into union with Christ and all the blessings Christ has accomplished.

Baptism Leads to Spirit and Church Reception

The archetypal baptism for all Christians is the baptism of Jesus in the river Jordan at the hands of John the Baptist. What happened? Unrecognized but important to the meaning of baptism is that this occurred in a very special location: the river Jordan. It is not at all pressing the details too much to say that John chose to baptize people in the place *where Israel* crossed the Jordan after being liberated from Egypt, received the law, wandered in the wilderness, and then by crossing the river entered the land. John and Jesus, by baptizing and being baptized at that very location, were dramatizing that God was about to rebegin Israel's life in the land. Hence, Jesus chose twelve apostles as Moses had appointed twelve tribal leaders for the land. More could be said but need not be here. What we learn is that *baptism is the beginning of a brand-new life.*[4]

When Jesus emerges from the water of the Jordan River, two profound moments occur: the Holy Spirit descends on Jesus for his messianic task, and the Father announces to all who can hear that this Jesus is none other than "my Son, whom I love; with him I am well pleased" (Matt. 3:17). The archetypal baptism then connects baptism to the ultimate approval of the Father as well as to the reception and empowering and anointing of the Holy Spirit. Baptism is about God announcing that the one baptized is God's child.

In his famous Pentecost sermon Peter promises this to those who repent and are baptized: "you will receive the gift of the Holy Spirit" (Acts 2:38). There are some debates about the order in which important dimensions of our redemption occur. Do we receive the Spirit prior to faith, at the moment of faith, or at our baptism? The New Testament doesn't seem to know or care, as the order varies from one text to another. We conclude that baptism is a complex event: Spirit reception, repentance, faith, confession, and baptism.[5] That debate aside, let us also not forget that Jesus himself connected the Spirit to baptism when he revealed to Nicodemus that we must be born both of "water and the Spirit" (John 3:5). Spirit reception and baptism then are connected.

To return for just a brief moment to how the Anglican baptismal liturgy proceeds, in the baptism service there comes a time when the pastor applies the "chrism," or consecrated oil. That is, each baptized person is anointed with oil. That oil embodies, enacts, and symbolizes the gift of the Holy Spirit. There is a long, long history in the church of chrismation, and in spite of debates about what happens in what order and about other topics related to anointing and baptism, once one learns about this history one might be forgiven for being disappointed at the absence of anointing with oil in many baptismal practices of Christian churches. Some seem to combine water baptism and chrismation by making the sign of the cross *with water* on the forehead of the person being baptized. But what chrismation emphasizes is what we have already seen in the baptismal verses in the Bible: the Spirit attends the baptism.[6] Many of us then urge our fellow Christians, "Bring back the oil!" Those who practice chrismation are in essence saying, "Bring in the Holy Spirit!" Do we realize that being anointed with oil is a way of saying we are "messianic"? That is, since the term "Christ" or "Messiah" means the anointed one, we become little christs and little messiahs when we too are anointed.

Now a very important additional observation: Paul tells us that "we were all baptized by one Spirit so as to form one body—whether Jews or Gentiles, slave or free—and we were all given the one Spirit to drink" (1 Cor. 12:13). Again, water baptism and Spirit are connected intimately in Paul's mind. The order may not be clear, but the connection is certain: in our baptism the Spirit comes on us. That observation then leads to this one: the one baptism of water and Spirit ushers us into the family of God, the church.[7] We are back to the beginning, then—back to the connection of the ritual of baptism, the family, and the church. Dietrich Bonhoeffer, in one of his essays on baptism, said this in more erudite terms: "Baptism is the actual consummated transfer of the human being into the church-community of the end times and incorporation into the body of Christ by means of a physical action instituted by Christ."[8]

This act of being transferred into the church is accomplished by the power of the Spirit.

It is a pity that in far too many Christian circles baptism has been radically separated from the gift of the Spirit. In such a separation, unfortunately, those Christians are departing from the Bible's own pattern, beginning with the archetypal baptism of Jesus. Whether or not one believes in anointing with oil, the promise of the Spirit in baptism deserves emphasis. What better way of communicating this can be found than chrismation, or anointing with oil?

Baptism Leads to Forgiveness and Redemption

The third theme is one that can raise the blood pressure of many of us. I confess it once raised mine. We Anglicans are Protestants with a touch (or more) of a Reformed understanding of the Protestant faith. That means that evangelical-type Anglicans are committed to the *solas* (Latin for the "alone" elements of our faith). One of my fellow worshipers at Church of the Redeemer, Kevin Vanhoozer, discussed each of the five *solas*—grace alone, faith alone, Scripture alone, Christ alone, for the glory of God alone—in a recent important study.[9] When our third theme then connects baptism to forgiveness and redemption, our heritage asks us to make things clear. Why? If salvation is by "grace alone" then we need to make sure we don't infringe on grace when we affirm a connection of baptism with forgiveness of sins—especially when we are discussing the baptism of infants.

Baptism is a church event, and redemption and faith are announced and promised as the church assembles around the person being baptized. If there is one thing clear about baptism texts in the Bible, though, it is that they often connect baptism to forgiveness. "Scripture alone" presses us to receive the connection. Genuine biblical faith connects baptism to redemption. The texts deserve to be quoted in order to make the point clear, and again, please read them closely:

> Peter replied, "Repent and be baptized, every one of you, in the name of Jesus Christ *for the forgiveness of your sins. And you will receive the gift of the Holy Spirit.*" (Acts 2:38)

> And now what are you waiting for? Get up, be baptized *and wash your sins away*, calling on his name. (Acts 22:16)

> For all of you who were baptized into Christ *have clothed yourselves with Christ.* (Gal. 3:27)

> And that is what some of you were. *But you were washed, you were sanctified, you were justified* in the name of the Lord Jesus Christ and by the Spirit of our God. (1 Cor. 6:11)

> We were therefore buried with him through baptism into death in order that, just as Christ was raised from the dead through the glory of the Father, we too may live a new life. For if we have been united with him in a death like his, we will certainly also be united with him in a resurrection like his. For we know that our old self was crucified with him so that the body ruled by sin might be done away with, that we should no longer be slaves to sin. (Rom. 6:4–6)

> He saved us, not because of righteous things we had done, but because of his mercy. *He saved us through the washing of rebirth and renewal by the Holy Spirit.* (Titus 3:5)

> Let us draw near to God with a sincere heart and with the full assurance that faith brings, having our hearts sprinkled

to cleanse us from a guilty conscience and having our bodies washed with pure water. (Heb. 10:22)

And this water symbolizes *baptism that now saves you also—* not the removal of dirt from the body but the pledge of a clear conscience toward God. It saves you by the resurrection of Jesus Christ. (1 Pet. 3:21)

Baptism is drawn so closely into the circle of salvation, or salvation so closely into the circle of baptism, that some of us need to admit discomfort. And I would add, as a committed Protestant, that being comfortable with the Bible needs to be dashed at times with some cold water, because God is always ready to speak forth a fresh word into the church of our day. What these verses make us uncomfortable with is something God wants us to see as true: baptism and redemption are closely connected. In these verses we have every reason once again to emphasize baptism as something God is doing. You can read these Bible verses backward and still get the same message. What we dare not do is avoid them, ignore them, or explain them away.

Sign, Seal, Symbol, Sacrament, and Seed

Of the three themes we have discussed—union with Christ, Spirit and church reception, and redemption—it is redemption that deserves the most careful explanation, and churches and theologians and creeds have done this using some very important terms. The church's best thinkers have landed on five major terms in defining what happens at baptism for our redemption: sign, seal, symbol, sacrament, and seed.

To call baptism a *sign* is to connect baptism to circumcision in the grand story of the Bible. Genesis 17:10–11 says, "Every male among you shall be circumcised. You are to undergo circumcision, and it will be *the sign* of the covenant between me and you." The Anglican Thirty-Nine Articles of Religion defines a sign as a "mark of difference," and baptism as a sign points us to the baptism of Christ—his death, burial, and resurrection. As such, baptism of an infant points us to Christ in the act of baptism itself.

Baptism is also a *seal*, and this too connects us to Abraham. The apostle Paul tells us that Abraham "received circumcision as a sign, *a seal* of the righteousness he had by faith while he was still uncircumcised" (Rom. 4:11). In speaking of baptism as a seal, we are saying that it completes faith and sets a seal of approval by God, the family, and the church on the person being baptized. Baptism is a visible word of God's grace and love for us. As a seal, it confirms the redemptive love of God on the child. That child who journeys into faith and is confirmed at confirmation puts a seal on the journey as he or she intentionally believes and enters into the faith of that baptism.

Baptism is also a *symbol*, which means it symbolizes and points to and illustrates something. What is that something? The grace of God, the love of God, and the redemptive covenant of God for us. Some limit baptism to (nothing more than) a symbol, but we believe baptism is not only symbolic but also a redemptive sign, seal, sacrament, and seed.

Baptism is a *sacrament*. What is a sacrament? The term refers to something that is holy, but the word's meaning gets a bit bigger than that. It is a rite, with created matter (water, bread, wine) and words that point us to God, and through that process sacraments become for us a means of grace. As the Thirty-Nine Articles of Religion defines them, "Sacraments ordained of Christ be not only badges or tokens of Christian men's profession, but rather they be certain sure witnesses, and effectual signs of grace, and God's good will towards us, by the which he doth work invisibly in us, and doth not only quicken, but also strengthen and confirm our Faith in him."[10] The Catechism of *The Book of Common Prayer* defines "sacrament" as follows:[11]

> Q: What are the sacraments?
> A: The sacraments are outward and visible signs of inward and spiritual grace, given by Christ as sure and certain means by which we receive that grace.

Garwood Anderson, professor of New Testament at the Anglican seminary called Nashotah House, reminded me of an oft-repeated way of defining a sacrament: a sign that effects (or produces) what it symbolizes.

Baptism with water and union with Christ, reception of the Spirit and church, and forgiveness are spiritually connected. That is, when we say baptism is a sacrament we declare that baptism when duly performed is a portal of grace into the person being baptized. The term "sacrament" is all but defined when we speak of baptism as a sign, a seal, and a seed. We believe something truly and redemptively happens to the child who is baptized. That child is launched into Christ, the Spirit, faith, the church, and redemption. The "something" that happens is perhaps best defined by the next word: "seed."

Baptism is a *seed*. That is, it is a seed of God's redemptive love and grace that is planted in the child in the context of the covenant-based family and church. As we have already explained, conversion is a journey that begins for the infant at baptism, during which a seed is planted—a seed that will grow. The baptism of an infant then is a seed of grace, of the Spirit, of faith, of public profession, and of discipleship. As a seed it is in need of water and sun, as Anglican evangelist and priest Michael Green has said so well: "Baptism is the pledge of

God's new life. But it is like a seed: it only germinates when it encounters the water of repentance and the sunshine of faith."[12]

Behind, under, before, and alongside those five terms is something else: baptism is *an act, an event, a physical rite, or ritual with water* in the presence of an authorized baptizer (a priest, a pastor, a deacon), a family, and a church fellowship. We enact, embody, and live out the covenant God has made with us whenever we baptize. Two crisp definitions of baptism come from Lars Hartman and Richard Pratt Jr. Hartman, who has himself written a scholarly study of baptism, defines baptism as an "earthly, concrete event [that] mediates divine actions and conveys spiritual gifts."[13] Pratt, an Old Testament professor, says when he describes the sacrament of baptism among the Reformed that "Reformed theology views baptism as a mysterious encounter with God that takes place through a rite involving physical elements and special ceremony."[14] One element is absent in both definitions: the family, surrounded by the church. So, I offer my own definition: baptism is a physical act (or rite) in water in which God mediates multiple blessings of grace to the one being baptized (in the context of family-centered church fellowship as a pledge to nurture the baptized into spiritual formation). Church historian and pastor Carl Trueman reminds us yet again that baptism is about what God is doing, not what we are doing: "It should be clear that baptism is first and foremost an act of God. God is the agent in baptism, not the priest or minister who applies the water and pronounces the Trinitarian formula."[15] To say it yet again: baptism is an act of God in which God does what only God can do. Is our focus on what we do or what we are qualified to do or how much faith we have, or is our focus on what God has done for us in Christ?

My definition of baptism above also makes room for the infant, but the question we need to ask is whether the Bible provides a ground for believing in infant baptism. You may recall that we have interrupted our discussion of the service of baptism for two chapters to examine the meaning of baptism and why infants are baptized. We will resume the baptism service when chapter 5 is complete, but what follows is for some the most important and difficult of the chapters.

5

The Bible
and Infant Baptism

We turn back to earlier discussions for an important reminder: the covenant formed with Abraham was located in his *family* because the family was central to all "religious" life in ancient Israel. It was not just Abraham who was circumcised. Abraham's son was as well. In ancient Israel, as in all religions of the Greek and Roman world, one did not choose one's religion. One's religion was inherited. Religion was something passed to one's children by way of culture, instruction, and family traditions. Surrounding that family was a community, a tribal region in the land of Israel, and a nation. Circumcision, then, was never a solo act by a solo father on a solo son. It was preeminently an act of a father on a son in the context of the father's own circumcision and in the context of a family, a community, and a nation. That son became not only part of the family but a potential functioning member of an entire nation. The swift cut of the knife authorized that child to be part of a community.

So, typical for the ancient world, and central to how God chose to work with Israel, the covenant God made with father Abraham became effective for his whole household, as it did for the rest of Israel's history. Children who grew up in Judaism didn't choose to join Judaism; they were already incorporated into Judaism from the day of their birth. Judaism then was a *household* covenant-based faith with the God of Israel, YHWH. The New Testament texts make it more than clear that *entire* households were baptized.

With that term we begin to enter the first reason for infant baptism. That very term "household" was an inclusive term, and in the New Testament we hear for the first time of the *baptism* of entire households.[1] The first and most important question about household baptism is this: What exactly was a household? Was it the house itself? The father only? The father and the mother? The father and anyone in the household who was old enough to believe and who did believe and repent? Everyone in and attached to the house, including slaves and servants and relatives and dependents? Ask this set of questions to anyone who knows the ancient world and you get this answer or something like it: a household included a father, his wife, his children, his or her siblings, his or her parents and grandparents and relatives, as well as domestic slaves and even the homeless who have been given shelter. Not all persons in the household, of course, had the same status or rights, but this point cannot be overemphasized: a household included everyone in the household![2] (I will discuss this below.)

Therefore, to baptize a *household* meant to baptize more than the new-covenant member, which in most cases was *the father or mother*. To baptize a household was to baptize everyone in the household. Everyone means everyone, not just some. We should also emphasize that the early Christian descriptions of household baptism would not have spoken of the baptism of a "household" *if only one person were being baptized or if only (adult) believers were being baptized*. In those cases, they would have said, "He and those in his household who believed were baptized." But this is not what the Bible says, and we have to let it tell us what to believe. The Bible itself, which is shaped from the beginning by a rich covenant-based theology of family as the focal center of covenant life, forces us to think, by using "household," that the faith of the initial believer renders the rest of the household fit for baptism. Why? Because the family is the nucleus of God's work in this world.

Back to the Covenant and the Family: Household Baptism

That there are texts in the New Testament connecting baptism to the household has been mentioned, so we must take a careful look at these texts—and again, read them carefully. The first one is often cited by those examining household baptisms, but it is not as clearly a case for household baptism as some of the other texts. What happens is that Peter has been talking to Cornelius, but suddenly, when baptisms occur, he begins using the plural "their" and "they."

> "Surely no one can stand in the way of *their* being baptized with water. *They* have received the Holy Spirit just as we have." So he ordered that *they* be baptized in the name of Jesus Christ. Then *they* asked Peter to stay with them for a few days. (Acts 10:47–48)

Some say the shift from Cornelius to "they" indicates that it was not only he but the entire household that was baptized.

There are good reasons to affirm this view because of the other examples of household baptism in the book of Acts. So we turn to the clearest examples of household baptism:

> When she *and the members of her household* were baptized, she invited us to her home. "If you consider me a believer in the Lord," she said, "come and stay at my house." And she persuaded us. (Acts 16:15)

> He then brought them out and asked, "Sirs, what must I do to be saved?" They replied, "Believe in the Lord Jesus, and you will be saved—*you and your household*." (Acts 16:30–31)

> Yes, I also baptized *the household of Stephanas*; beyond that, I don't remember if I baptized anyone else. (1 Cor. 1:16)

A final instance emphasizes that others in the household believed:

> Crispus, the synagogue leader, and *his entire household believed in the Lord*; and many of the Corinthians who heard Paul believed and were baptized. (Acts 18:8)

This must be said firmly: it is well-nigh (and I would say it *is*) impossible for this many households to be baptized and for there not to be any children or infants in the household. Households were too large and too encompassing for them to be absent.[3] What is more, the New Testament *explicitly* states that not only a specific person—Crispus, Stephanas, and others—but also their entire household was baptized.[4] A leader of the house entails the whole household participating in that leader's faith and religion.

There was nothing unusual about this in the world of the New Testament, but some are not aware of the family- and father-based nature of ancient religions. Inclusion of the household in a parent's, especially a father's, religion or faith was common in the Roman world, including in the culture of the early church. In the Roman Empire a child's religion was determined not by some choice in the teenage years but by that child's family. Religion and nation and family were all but indistinguishable. In rare cases when a parent chose to be involved in another religious practice, that parent inevitably drew the rest of the household, especially their children, into the new religious practices. No one would have been surprised when Stephanas had his children baptized. What would have been surprising would have been Stephanas choosing *not* to baptize his children and his wife and his household! Again, this is not just Roman Empire practice; this is fully Jewish as well. To repeat, parents circumcised their boys on the eighth day, and circumcision was how that child entered into the covenant, the family, the community, and the nation. When a gentile converted to Judaism, that gentile often enough had other males in the family circumcised. Every Jew thus was entitled to participation in the covenant on the basis of his or her parents' covenant membership. Every convert to Judaism entered into the covenant through a process that included both circumcision and almost certainly "first Passover" (to imitate the language of "first Communion"). Baptism needs to be located in the centrality of the family, and once it is it becomes household baptism.

Consider this, too, from the early church: It may be hard to date the *Apostolic Tradition*, attributed traditionally to Hippolytus, with precision since it also reflects traditions that were passed on in the early church, but we are wise to date it in the second or third century. What this early Christian tradition about the baptism service reveals is that the church baptized children who could not yet speak for themselves.[5] First we hear of an Easter service and the specification for pure water:

> At the hour in which the cock crows, they shall first pray over the water. When they come to the water, the water shall be pure and flowing, that is, the water of a spring or a flowing body of water.

A practice long since abandoned was that anointing with oil and baptism, like the baptism of converts in the Jewish world at the time and not unlike typical anointings and washings in Roman baths, was undertaken naked so that the whole body would be cleansed.[6] This meant, naturally, that baptisms were led by bishops or pastors and occurred in groups for whom the nudity would be appropriate (boys with men, girls with women, women with women, and men with men) or, alternatively, in private:

> Then they shall take off all their clothes.

The image of stripping off one's clothing in the New Testament—found in texts such as Ephesians 4:22, 24; Colossians 3:8–10; and 1 Peter 2:1; see also 1 Peter 3:21—is perceived by many today as reflecting the early Christian practice of disrobing and then being robed in white after the baptism. It comes as no surprise then that after stripping off we read of "putting on" new clothing (Rom. 13:12, 14; Gal. 3:27; Eph. 6:11–17; Col. 3:12; 1 Pet. 4:1). This disrobing and re-robing language may well reflect the habits of baptism in the earliest churches.[7]

Now we come to the three groups to be baptized, beginning with children, followed by men, and then women. The children include those who can speak for themselves and those who cannot. In the latter case, the parents or another family member would speak on their behalf.

> The children shall be baptized first. All of the children who can answer for themselves, let them answer. If there are any children who cannot answer for themselves, let their parents answer for them, or someone else from their family.

> After this, the men will be baptized.

> Finally [with the men now out of the baptistery for the sake of modesty], the women, after they have unbound their hair, and removed their jewelry. No one shall take any foreign object with themselves down into the water.[8]

To be sure, this is not first century, and it is not New Testament. But it is early Christian tradition, and there is no sign that baptizing infants was an innovation or that some thought baptizing infants was impermissible. Remember what was said by Origen: "The Church received *from the apostles* the tradition of giving baptism even to infants" (*Commentary on Romans* 5.9, emphasis added).[9] Rather, this looks like church tradition that was being passed on as the way things were done. *It Takes a Church to Baptize*, as the reader knows, is organized around the liturgy of baptism, and all churches today that baptize infants use a liturgy rooted in the *Apostolic Tradition.*[10]

If we return to the New Testament texts about household baptisms, we see that one of these texts, Acts 18:8, says the "entire household believed," but the other texts rarely give any indication of the presence of the household's faith; instead, they suggest rather calmly and firmly that the faith of the *paterfamilias* led to the baptism of the rest of the household. Yes, it is clear that no infant or unbelieving child is mentioned explicitly, but the very term "household" implies corporate union with the act of the father and therefore entails the baptism of all in that household, and *surely at least one of these households had at least one child or infant*. I repeat: had the emphasis been on "only believer's baptism," then the New Testament texts would have said so. That the Bible says a "household" was baptized means the faith of one establishes the baptisms of others. There would be no other reason to use this particular word. It all hangs on the meaning of the term "household."

After a painstaking study of "household" in the Old Testament and Jewish sources, the great German New Testament historian Joachim Jeremias concluded, "The picture is always the same. The phrase 'he and his (whole) house' denotes the complete family; normally husband, wife and children. In no single case is the term 'house' restricted to the adult members of the house, though on the other hand children alone may be mentioned when the whole house is meant."[11]

Two observations rise to the surface from these New Testament texts: (1) The New Testament, like the Old Testament, believes the parent's faith incorporates children of that parent into the faith community. Whereas the Old Testament incorporated sons through circumcision, the New Testament incorporates male and female children through baptism. (2) It is next to impossible historically for this many households to be baptized without any children or infants. J. I. Packer has accurately observed that "it is unrealistic, if not actually evasive, to suppose that when the apostles and others baptized households . . . there were no very young children in any of the families."[12] These Bible verses make it highly likely, and almost certain, that infants and children were baptized along with the father or mother of the family when the latter first believed and were baptized.[13] Faith, then, is required for baptism, but it may be the faith of the adult convert along with his or her sponsor, or the faith of the parents and godparents, and even more the faith of the surrounding church.

When we at Church of the Redeemer surround the infant, the parents, and family and friends, we are acting in faith as a community of faith. The faith of the baptized (or her or his parents) is not a solo faith; it is a faith with others. A wonderful New Testament scholar of the previous generation, Oscar Cullmann, in a breath of fresh personal air in his book on baptism, made a similar confession about his own "baptismal faith": "My baptismal faith is not simply faith in Christ's work in general but on the quite specific deed which he performed upon me at the moment of my Baptism in my being received into the inner circle of his Kingdom, that is, into his earthly Body."[14] This is the way a family-based and covenant-based church understands the faith of the baptized.

Infant baptism, to circle back to only brief remarks already made, is an act of God in the context of the family, and that is why it gets connected in the New Testament to the premier family act of circumcision. I want now to take a closer look at this topic. Why? The New Testament explicitly connects Christian baptism with Jewish circumcision.

Circumcision as a Memorial of the Covenant

Anglicans are convinced about baptizing infants for a variety of reasons, one of which is the family-covenant context of faith in the Bible. Another reason comes to the surface now concerning the overt analogy of circumcision and baptism in the Bible itself. The topic of circumcision has been mentioned already, but it is time for us to dig more deeply into what the Bible teaches.

The original act of circumcision was a sign of the covenant between YHWH and Abraham,[15] and that sign was then extended to his children.[16] In Genesis 15 Abraham is justified by faith, and in Genesis 17:11 (sealed with the rite as the "sign of the covenant"[17]) he accepts the sign of the covenant, circumcision. As a result of this new sign of the covenant, Abraham circumcises his son Isaac at eight days (Gen. 21:4). This is how God instructed Abraham to incorporate his children into the covenant-based faith. This becomes the pattern in Israel, and it is the pattern inherited by Jesus and the apostles.

As circumcision was the "entry rite" into the covenant God made with Israel, so baptism is the entry rite into the new covenant God makes with the church. This comparison forms a very important structural parallel, and it concerns first-generation believers and their children:

A   Abraham believed and was justified and then circumcised.
 B   Abraham the believer circumcised his son to *enter him into the same covenant.*

A′ Christians in the New Testament believe and are justified and then baptized.
 B′ Therefore it follows that, as with Abraham and his children, so with New Testament believers and their families: *the children of believers are entered into the same covenant* through an analogous initiatory rite—namely, infant baptism.

If God entered Abraham into the covenant by circumcision and demanded Abraham enter his son through circumcision, then it is clear that God thinks the best way to form children into the covenant faith is by way of birthright entrance into the covenant. I cannot emphasize this enough: this is God's way. It follows then in the Christian faith that first-generation believers will undergo adult baptism and then enter their children through a birthright rite of entry—infant baptism. No one in the New Testament or early church ever questioned this process of formation. One has to think that the God of the covenant with Abraham is the God of the new covenant, and if it was God's pattern then it is at least reasonable and theologically consistent to think that God's pattern in the new covenant would be the same.

We need to look a little more closely at how covenants are described in the Bible because they will help us understand what a baptism is, and what we are about to see is that the baptism of an infant memorializes what God has done for us in Christ. This discussion requires some intense concentration on the special terms used for covenant circumcision in the Bible. The first expression, "sign of the covenant," is found in Genesis 17:11; the Hebrew term behind this phrase is *ot berit*. Here is what we read in the Bible: "You [Abraham] are to undergo circumcision, and it will be the *sign of the covenant* between me and you." This same term (*ot*, "sign") is used elsewhere in the Pentateuch for the rainbow (Gen. 9:12–13), sabbath (Exod. 31:13), and redemption of the firstborn (Exod. 13:16). Each of these great moments in Israel's history is understood as a redemptive act of God. Furthermore, the *ot* or "sign of the covenant" looks back to *memorialize* God's wonderful redemptive act. A covenant and a repetition of that covenant ritual then is a supreme act of remembrance. The sign of the covenant functions as a sacrament of memory, a sacrament of what God did long ago. It is a sign of something God does and not a sign of something we do.

Knowing that a covenant is a memorial allows us to jump ahead for a moment to reimagine what baptism is. I want to suggest this for your serious consideration: a baptism is concerned to signify or seal not simply or even primarily the *present believer's faith* but the believer's participation in the *remembrance* of the grand covenant act. The new covenant's formal event is the life, death, burial, and resurrection/ascension of Jesus, so a new-covenant baptism memorializes the life, death, burial, and resurrection/ascension of Jesus. We need then to remind ourselves that baptisms are not supremely or exclusively about us or about "my" faith or even "our" faith but about Jesus and his baptism. Our baptisms are designed to focus everyone's attention on Jesus and his baptism and what God did in him to establish the new covenant. Baptisms thus do not simply *look at the now*, but instead our baptisms supremely and primarily *remember the past.*

Kris and I have been to Pearl Harbor Memorial and Punchbowl Memorial, both in Honolulu, and each was beyond a stunning experience. At Pearl Harbor and at Punchbowl, what happens? The United States has created memorials by using original pieces and relics from World War II, monuments, and gravestone markers, as well as movies, pictures, plaques, and timelines. It is impossible, at least for me, to wander through Pearl Harbor or Punchbowl without entering imaginatively into the Japanese invasion of Pearl Harbor, the tragic scenes of war that always include death and bravery, and without wanting to learn more—and my way of learning more is to read a book. I read *The Day of Infamy* and entered more deeply into the memorial of our nation at war. That's what memorials do— they remember a solemn act or event, establish physical objects as the means of entry into the past, and take us back in order to fill our hearts with history, hope, purpose, and meaning.

Though of a different kind and of a supernatural order, both circumcision and baptism are memorials of what God did in the past: the covenant with Abraham and the redemption through Jesus's life, death, burial, and resurrection.

Another term is used for the family-covenant rite of circumcision God made with Abraham. Romans 4:11 uses the word "sign" (*sēmeion*) for covenant circumcision and then defines it as a "seal" (*sphragis*):[18] "And he received circumcision as a sign, *a seal of the righteousness* that he had by faith while he was still uncircumcised. So then, he is the father of all who believe but have not been circumcised, in order that righteousness might be credited to them." A sign points to something, it reveals something, it marks something as distinct, and at the same time a sign vouches for and pledges that the contents of a covenant are authentic. The seal is God's promise to make good on his promise to Abraham; a seal confirms and reminds us of God's gracious love for us. Most importantly, by understanding a covenant as a "sign," we are drawn once again into an act—circumcision—that *looks back at* and *memorializes* the covenant God made with Abraham.[19] When Isaac was circumcised, that act looked back to Abraham's circumcision and to the covenant God was making with Abraham. A sign confirms that the act is a memorial.

If this is the case, then infant baptism is not simply a pledge of the parents and the church of the *future faith* of that child but is first of all *a memorial of what Christ has done and the entrance of that infant into those salvific events* as an act of faith on the part of all. It is less about that child's faith and more about pledging that child to new-creation life through Christ's death and resurrection. It is a sign and memorial of the baptism of Christ himself as his own entry into his death and resurrection. If a covenant is a memorial, then a baptism is also a memorial. But how is circumcision connected to baptism? We had to discuss covenant as memorial before we could turn to the texts that connect circumcision to baptism.

Circumcision and Baptism

If we are going to baptize infants, we will want to do so because we see circumcision fulfilled in baptism. This is what we mean by the "big ideas" and a theology of baptism in the Bible. If baptism fulfills circumcision, what was done in Abraham's day to his sons (circumcision) would be done in our day to infants (baptism). To draw this out just a bit, Abraham's faith led to circumcision, and then by divine direction he circumcised his son, who did not yet have faith. Hence, the faith of the father obtained for the son, and that faith of the father was to nurture the faith of the son so that Isaac would grow into the same kind of faith as Abraham. So too with baptism: the adult believer is baptized, and from then on the children of that believer are circumcised as the beginning of those children's covenant faith formation. Once again, notice the importance of the family to covenant faith, and notice even more the priority of God's grace in covenant circumcision and baptism.

The Bible ties baptism to circumcision explicitly. In Colossians 2, circumcision in the old covenant is tied by Paul to baptism in the new covenant.[20] Read these two verses carefully:

> In him you were also *circumcised* with a *circumcision* not performed by human hands. Your whole self ruled by the flesh was put off when you were *circumcised by Christ*, having been buried with him *in baptism*, in which you were also raised with him through your faith in the working of God, who raised him from the dead. (vv. 11–12)[21]

Paul makes a very typical Old Testament move: the physical rite of circumcision requires as well a deeper circumcision of the heart. This is why Moses in the Old Testament promised that when the exile was over, God "will circumcise your hearts and the hearts of your descendants, so that you may love him with all your heart and with all your soul, and live" (Deut. 30:6). It sure seems the apostle Paul thinks that promise is fulfilled when he says they were "circumcised by Christ." The next step is to tie spiritual circumcision to baptism. Paul does this when he draws together the two—the physical and the spiritual circumcision—and so connects circumcision to baptism. To quote Paul again: "Your whole self ruled by the flesh was put off when you were *circumcised by Christ*, having been buried with him *in baptism*." The physical-now-spiritual ritual of circumcision has become the physical-now-spiritual act of baptism. The connection of circumcision to baptism leads to what theologians throughout the church's history have believed: what was the case with circumcision is now the case with baptism. If a physical-spiritual circumcision is the Old Testament version of New Testament baptism, which is also a physical-spiritual act, Paul cannot be far from suggesting or teaching that just as circumcision was applied to a child, so too should baptism be.

Why say this? Circumcision was applied to *every person in the covenant person's household*. Notice that in Genesis 17:23 circumcision applies to Ishmael, who is not the son of the covenant (that would be Isaac) but the son of the servant woman whom Abraham thought he could use to create the fulfillment of God's promise for offspring:

> On that very day Abraham took his son Ishmael and *all those born in his household or bought with his money, every male in his household*, and circumcised them, as God told him.

Moses later says in Exodus 12:44, 48:

> *Any slave* you have bought may eat [the Passover meal] after
> you have circumcised him.

> A *foreigner residing among you* who wants to celebrate the
> LORD's Passover must have *all the males in his household cir-*
> *cumcised*; then he may take part like one born in the land. No
> uncircumcised male may eat it.

In the Old Testament, I want to repeat, there is a much deeper circumcision, a circumcision of the heart, and heart-circumcision
is redemptive (Deut. 10:16; Jer. 4:4). Thus, in Deuteronomy
30:6 we read:

> The Lord your God *will circumcise your hearts and the hearts*
> *of your descendants*, so that you may love him with all your
> heart and with all your soul, and live.

In the Colossians 2 passage, Paul draws the rites of both
circumcision and baptism into the heart and draws the heart
into the rites. The connection and fulfillment of circumcision
in baptism supports a covenant entrance of the child into the
church family, and at the same time he expects the baptized
person to be baptized in the heart as well. Here is how the
apostle Paul puts it with respect to circumcision (and therefore
baptism): "No, a person is a Jew who is one inwardly; and
circumcision is circumcision of the heart, by the Spirit, not
by the written code" (Rom. 2:29). Baptism, likewise, is not a
physical rite only but is also the sign of a covenant in the heart.

The early church theologians connected circumcision to baptism and saw the latter as the fulfillment of the former. Justin
Martyr, already in the second century, speaks of baptism as "our

circumcision" (*Dialogue with Trypho* 19). Cyril of Jerusalem, in the fourth century, says of Abraham, "And then, following upon our faith, we receive like him the spiritual seal, being circumcised by the Holy Spirit through baptism, not in the foreskin of the body, but in the heart" (*Catechetical Lectures* 5.6). Not long after Cyril, Augustine urged that baptisms occur on the eighth day after birth, just as circumcisions occurred on the eighth day.[22]

Though the connection is first made by Paul, the early church caught on and developed it. Many today take Paul at his word and offer insights into baptism in light of circumcision. Methodist New Testament scholar Ben Witherington III offers a fresh and reasonable summary of what is taught in Colossians 2:11–12: "For Paul, what water baptism symbolizes is close to what circumcision meant, and from Colossians 2 it is hard not to believe that Paul saw water baptism as in one sense the Christian's circumcision. Probably he saw baptism as a rite of passage similar to, but replacing, circumcision, which was the sign of an earlier, and now defunct, covenant."[23]

Evangelical Anglican theologian Michael Bird says it crisply:

> What circumcision anticipates, baptism celebrates. The covenant sign of circumcision in the Abrahamic covenant is replaced with baptism as the symbol for the new covenant.[24]

> What is more, if the new covenant is the eschatological fulfillment of the Abrahamic covenant and if the Abrahamic covenant had a place for children, how much more so should the new covenant have a place for children.[25]

The best reading of Colossians 2 is that it connects the rite of physical-spiritual circumcision as a rite of entry with the rite of entry in the new covenant: water baptism.

Many of us remain concerned with the importance of personal faith for anyone who is baptized as an infant. We are concerned that infant baptism will not lead to personal faith. This concern is not resolved by fighting against infant baptism and then fighting for adult baptism. After all, there are plenty of those who were baptized upon profession of faith who have nothing to do with God, with faith in Christ, with discipleship, or with the church. Rather than saying the importance of faith means not baptizing infants, the concern with the importance of growing into personal faith is addressed by evangelism and, even more, the family's capacity to nurture one into faith, as I have been observing from the very start of this book. The same concern is also addressed by giving more attention to conversion as a process, one that begins in many with infant baptism. One can study the history of those who baptize infants and those who baptize adults and discover that the most "success" can be found not on the basis of who baptizes adults or who baptizes infants but on the basis of who disciples children well. Infant baptizers who take the formation of their family seriously are just as likely to produce believing adults as are adult baptizers who take spiritual formation seriously. In this discussion, however, let us not lose contact with something more important: baptism is an act of God, not something we do or something we are worthy of by our faith. Rather, baptism is God's grace offered to us.

I contend that adult baptizers need to reconsider something else: there is today (at times) a *diminishment* of the family as the context of covenant participation and spiritual formation when it comes to strong defenses of believer's baptism. I will avoid mentioning the names of specific books, but I am not afraid to say that this diminishment applies to nearly all of those who defend believer's baptism. The family often doesn't even get mentioned, and when it does it is not as central as the Bible makes it. What also needs to be considered is that modernity's emphasis on the centrality of the individual ego makes covenant by way of kinship and family doubly difficult. Good covenant-centered theologians[26] connect covenant to family and to church. In connecting covenant to family and to church (or Israel), as we have already observed, covenant theologians are standing behind a very serious big idea in the Bible.[27]

Let me summarize what we have discovered so far in this chapter on infant baptism:

1. That household baptisms almost certainly included the baptism of infants

2. That the analogy of circumcision and baptism made by Paul in Colossians 2 indicates that baptism is the fulfillment of the circumcision

3. That if we accept household baptisms as including infants then it is quite reasonable to think the baptism-circumcision analogy of Paul included the baptism of infants already in New Testament times

Is there any more about this in the New Testament? Before we return to the Church of the Redeemer (Jay and Amanda are awaiting our return in the service of Holy Baptism) and the baptism of infants in the liturgy of the Anglican Church, I want to consider a text that almost certainly indicates that infants were baptized in the early church.

The Sanctity of the Children of Believers

The text that for many of us seals confidence that the early church baptized infants is 1 Corinthians 7:14:[28] "For the unbelieving

husband has been sanctified through his wife, and the unbelieving wife has been sanctified through her believing husband.
Otherwise your children would be unclean, but as it is, *they are
holy.*" The verse is sometimes brushed over in our quick reading of 1 Corinthians, a letter that bristles with at least three
problems per page. But let's pause to think over this verse and
ask how or why Paul thinks the children of believers are holy.

What does that term "holy" mean? Long discussion made
short: The word "holy" describes a person who is devoted, dedi-
cated, surrendered or offered to God, and because it describes
someone who is in the presence of God, it further describes a
person or thing now "separated from the world." Those devoted
to God are undevoted to the world; those who are offered to
God are withdrawn from use in the world. The term "holy"
thus means dedication into the presence of God, which leads to
separation from the world. Paul thinks the children of believers
are devoted to God; in fact, he thinks they have been brought
into the presence of God and therefore separated from the
world and its systemic sinfulness. Notice, too, that Paul thinks
an unbelieving spouse is also holy. The term "holy" here thus
describes what happens to those in a household baptism: they
are ushered into the presence of the holy God. Paul thinks
there is a special sanctity for anyone in a believer's household.[29]
(Once again, we are back to seeing the family's importance in
faith development.)

It is at this point that a question deserves to be asked: How
did the children become holy? Was it simply by virtue of the
parent's faith, or was there perhaps a baptism for the whole
household that included them? That is, was there a ceremony,
a rite, an analogous action to circumcision in the old covenant?

Our cumulative argument so far indicates that households
with children and infants were baptized. Just as in the old

covenant folks circumcised their sons, so the new-covenant Christians baptized their children. It is entirely reasonable to think that these children were washed or baptized in the name of Jesus or, at the least, that they participated through a parent or both parents in their baptisms as their familial representative. Paul is a Jew, and for Jews the word "holy" was central to their understanding of what was worthy of God's presence. As a Jew he was a man of rituals and rites. So I have a hard time thinking that in a ritual-rich world such as first-century Judaism or the Roman world there was no rite that led to the new status of the child. It is then entirely reasonable to think that calling a child "holy" entailed some kind of entrance rite—and if there was such a rite, it was baptism.

Therefore, if we consider household baptisms, the importance of families in the covenant, and the analogy with circumcision, then the presence of the term "holy" for infants or children in 1 Corinthians 7:14 is no surprise. The children of believers are sanctified—devoted to God's very presence—by the faith of their parents and the ritual of infant baptism. To adapt the words of Peter: "Surely no one can stand in the way of their being baptized with water" (Acts 10:47). Surely, I would add, either the step to infant baptism is very short or we are already there! Perhaps this is precisely what Peter meant when he said at the end of his famous sermon on the day of Pentecost that "the promise is for you *and your children*" (Acts 2:39). Why did Peter include children in this promise? Because faith is family- and covenant-based. Let's add one more question: Why did the apostle Paul, when he wrote to the churches in Ephesus and Colossae, include children in his instructions about how to live (Eph. 6:1–3; Col. 3:20)? Why did the apostle John write to children (1 John 2:12, 14)? Because from the outset the earliest churches incorporated their children into the faith. Once again, in a ritual-soaked world it is more than probable that some event occurred to mark the transition of these children from the world into the loving, protective care of God. Infant baptism is how that transition occurred.

John Calvin, one of the most influential Christian theologians in history and at the heart of the Reformation, agrees. In his *Institutes of the Christian Religion*, we read, "For this same reason, the children of Christians are considered holy; and even though born with only one believing parent, by the apostle's testimony they differ from the unclean seed of idolaters [1 Cor. 7:14]." How did this happen? Calvin continues: "Now seeing that the Lord, immediately after making the covenant with Abraham, commanded it to be sealed in infants by an outward sacrament [Gen. 17:12], what excuse will Christians give for not testifying and sealing it in their children today?"[30] Another Reformed theologian, Presbyterian Bryan Chapell, puts it like this: "Few verses in Scripture more forcefully indicate that God communicates his grace to children while they are in the household of a covenant parent," and it is the case that "while children remain under the authority of a believing parent, they are covenantally represented by that parent's faith."[31] Anglican Michael Bird adds his thoughts: "It is impossible to regard children as covenantally holy in their family if their entire family is not in fact integrated into the covenant of grace (see 1 Cor. 7:14)."[32] He is referring here to infant baptism.[33]

I have digressed in the last two chapters because so many who are considering becoming Anglican came to faith and were nurtured in baptistic cultures. They love our liturgy, they love the emphasis on Communion (we call it "Eucharist"), and they love the lectionary's emphasis on reading the Bible aloud when we gather for worship. But they have doubts about infant baptism, and as my friend Ethan McCarthy has reminded me, their doubts often are about sacraments and church, and hence I have devoted these two chapters to those who are asking whether infant baptism is biblical. I contend not only that it is biblical but that it is the most consistent way to embody our covenant- and family-based faith.

Let's return to Jay and Amanda.

6

The Act of Baptism

When we interrupted the Anglican service of Holy Baptism at the end of chapter 3, we had looked at the presentation and the three very serious commitments of the church, the parents, and the baptized. Following these, our priest had offered a prayer, and at this moment the official rite of baptism is performed.

It begins with a blessing over the water, not unlike the Old Testament's constant prayers and blessings over sacrifices in the temple. For some, such actions may smack of idolatry or ritual that perhaps turns them off. But the Bible's emphasis is a whole-body spirituality and a whole-creation redemption and a building-based, utensil-shaped, and ritual-ordered worship in the temple. The Anglican blessing of the water demonstrates a belief that what we do in the body and what kind of space we create for worship matters, that what God has created matters, and that this water is being devoted to God and separated from all other water on earth. Our priest draws us back into participating in the baptism:

Celebrant: The Lord be with you.

People: And also with you.

Celebrant: Let us give thanks to the Lord our God.

People: It is right to give him thanks and praise.

Then the celebrant prays the prayer that follows—but don't pass it by. This prayer brings into fresh expression the role of water in the Bible's story, and I have added numbers to make the biblical theme even more clear. The three themes of water in this prayer are creation, exodus, and the baptism of Jesus into his death and resurrection.

> We thank you, Almighty God, for the gift of water. (1) Over it the Holy Spirit moved in the beginning of creation. (2) Through it you led the children of Israel out of their bondage in Egypt into the land of promise. (3) In it your Son Jesus received the baptism of John and was anointed by the Holy Spirit as the Messiah, the Christ, to lead us, through his death and resurrection, from the bondage of sin into everlasting life.

We could also include another instance of water as a biblical theme between creation and the Red Sea crossing in the exodus—namely, the flood. Not only does Peter connect baptism to Noah (1 Pet. 3:20–21), but the early church commonly connected the waters of Noah's flood with baptism.[1]

After this prayer, the priest turns to God in thanksgiving for the water in the sanctuary as it is now connected to creation, exodus, and the baptism of Christ. The priest offers these words of thanksgiving for *our* baptism. Why *ours* or "we"? Because this baptism is a *memorial* of Christ's baptism, a *sign of the covenant* that points us to Christ's own baptism, his own death, and his own resurrection, and therefore it is the common rite of entrance for all who are gathered in Christ's name for this baptism. Because "we" have been baptized, we bring others to the blessings of this water.

> We thank you, Father, for the water of Baptism. In it we are buried with Christ in his death. By it we share in his resurrection. Through it we are reborn by the Holy Spirit. Therefore in joyful obedience to your Son, we bring into his fellowship those who come to him in faith, baptizing them in the Name of the Father, and of the Son, and of the Holy Spirit.

The priest then places his or her fingers into the basin of water and prays a blessing over it:

> Now sanctify this water, we pray you, by the power of your Holy Spirit, that those who here are cleansed from sin and born again may continue for ever in the risen life of Jesus Christ our Savior. To him, to you, and to the Holy Spirit, be all honor and glory, now and for ever. Amen.

One of the big themes of baptism in the New Testament, as we have outlined already, is that the Holy Spirit and baptism are connected. In the history of baptizing people in the church this connection comes to expression in chrismation, or the use of oil, discussed above in chapter 4.[2] Our priest proceeds by blessing the oil to be used on those who are baptized:

> Eternal Father, whose blessed Son was anointed by the Holy Spirit to be the Savior and servant of all, we pray you to consecrate this oil, that those who are sealed with it may share in the royal priesthood of Jesus Christ; who lives and reigns with you and the Holy Spirit, for ever and ever. Amen.

It took us until this point for the baptism to occur, but this time of preparation mirrors what needs to happen inside us as we prepare ourselves—the believing, baptized community—for nothing less than our welcoming of a new person into our church community and making a commitment to nurture that child in the faith. Here is how *The Book of Common Prayer* defines what is to happen:

> Each candidate is presented by name to the Celebrant, or to an assisting priest or deacon, who then immerses, or pours water upon, the candidate, saying
>
> [Name], I baptize you in the Name of the Father, and of the Son, and of the Holy Spirit. Amen.

If you are not skipping the bits that are quotations from the liturgy of baptism, you noticed that the priest "then immerses, or pours water upon, the candidate." This is one of the watery moments that have divided the church, so let me offer a brief word of clarification. The Greek word *baptizein* that stands behind our word "baptize" usually describes something that is immersed, dipped, or dunked in water. Jews immersed themselves totally into a *mikvah*, which is Hebrew for a sacred pool of water, used for ritual purification. John the Baptist baptized Jesus and others in the Jordan River, and one is justified in thinking he immersed such persons—or at least that they entered into the river and immersed themselves at his direction. Many have argued from this that all baptisms must be immersions. But imagery connected to baptism—as in having the Spirit poured on us or being baptized with fire—is not so easily connected to being plunged, dipped, or immersed.[3]

Yes, the baptism of Jesus was by immersion, and probably most adult baptisms were immersions. But already in the late first century or early second century Christians were given options on the method or mode of baptism.[4] An early Christian text called Didache says, "Baptize in the name of the Father and of the Son and of the Holy Spirit, in running water. But if you do not have running water, baptize in some other water. And if you cannot baptize in cold water, use warm. But if you have neither, *pour water on the head* three times in the name of Father and Son and Holy Spirit."[5] The Anglican Communion therefore permits some variance. While some may prefer immersion for an adult (and even for a child), others think it is more reasonable to pour water over the person three times. Our priest, Canon Jay Greener, pours water over the head of the person (adult or child) three times: in the name of the Father, the Son, and the Holy Spirit. Amen.

To return then from this brief excursus about the mode of baptism: the service of Holy Baptism continues with the priest's prayer for each person being baptized, even if it is a group of persons:

Heavenly Father, we thank you that by water and the Holy Spirit you have bestowed upon these your servants the forgiveness of sin, and have raised them to the new life of grace. Sustain them, O Lord, in your Holy Spirit. Give them an inquiring and discerning heart, the courage to will and to persevere, a spirit to know and to love you, and the gift of joy and wonder in all your works. Amen.

An alternative approach is found in *Common Worship*, where the priest speaks to the one being baptized the following words:

May God, who has received you by baptism into his Church, pour upon you the riches of his grace, that within the company of Christ's pilgrim people you may daily be renewed by his anointing Spirit, and come to the inheritance of the saints in glory.

The congregation affirms these words with "Amen," and the chrismation follows according to these directives:

Then the Bishop or Priest places a hand on the person's head, marking on the forehead the sign of the cross [using Chrism[6] if desired] and saying to each one

[Name], you are sealed by the Holy Spirit in Baptism and marked as Christ's own for ever. Amen.

Over and over I have emphasized that it takes a church and a family to baptize a person. For this baptism to be what it is meant to be—and you cannot deny that "Christ's own for ever" is a robust promise, just as circumcision was in the old covenant—the whole church, including all the ordained and the church members as well as sponsors, godparents, and family and friends, must commit to nurturing one another in the faith. This child being welcomed is receiving promises from all those in the sanctuary that they will be godly Christian influences and mentors and pastors for that child (or the person being baptized). All that has been said so far has been summarized in a classically pregnant set of expressions by J. I. Packer:

In infant baptism we consecrate young children to God, commit them by proxy to thoroughgoing adult Christianity, ask God to bring this about, and administer to them God's own covenant

sign, seal and bond of this full adult relationship. Believing that
our actions accord with his will, and that he is a faithful, loving, prayer-answering God, we trust that he has now received
the children covenantally and in some way started the work
in them that we have asked him to do; so, we finally pray that
the children will be led on from regeneration thus begun into
fullness of faith and faithfulness.[7]

As the service draws to a conclusion, the priest turns to the
entire church and says, "Let us welcome the newly baptized."
(At Church of the Redeemer we clap at this point, but I'm not
sure what is done in other churches. Some people are accus-
tomed to containing their joy with immobility.) Together we
offer the next words in the service:

> We receive you into the household of God. Confess the faith
> of Christ crucified, proclaim his resurrection, and share with
> us in his eternal priesthood.[8]

This is usually accompanied by joyful sniffling for some, by a
fullness of joy reflected on the face in others. One can see the
families ever so proud (and the infant who has just been baptized
either agitated or curious about something Jay is wearing, or
just glad to be back in the arms of mom or dad).

In our church we then celebrate the Eucharist with all those
who come to the Table. During that celebration of the Eucharist
we say the Lord's Prayer and sing together, and the service ends
with these beautiful and theologically rich prayers:

> All praise and thanks to you, most merciful Father, for adopting
> us as your own children, for incorporating us into your holy
> Church, and for making us worthy to share in the inheritance
> of the saints in light; through Jesus Christ your Son our Lord,

who lives and reigns with you and the Holy Spirit, one God, for ever and ever. Amen.

Almighty God, the Father of our Lord Jesus Christ, from whom every family in heaven and earth is named, grant you to be strengthened with might by his Holy Spirit, that, Christ dwelling in your hearts by faith, you may be filled with all the fullness of God. Amen.

Yes, the motto of Anglicanism is *lex orandi, lex credendi*: the law of prayer is the law of belief. In what I have so far sketched I have simply followed the order of worship so it can be seen for what it accomplishes: it shapes what we all learn to believe, just as those children in the novels of Marilynne Robinson and Harper Lee learned their theology by attendance at church.

As we prepare to depart, we anticipate the commission from our curate, Amanda:

Celebrant: Go forth into the world, rejoicing in the power of the Spirit.

You and I: Thanks be to God!

The exclamation point after "God" brings to finality what has been said over and over in this book: baptism is the act of God's grace to us, so we are driven to exclaim our thanks to God.

7

My Personal Testimony

At times my own story has risen to the surface for a moment in *It Takes a Church to Baptize*, but it might be helpful to some for me to sort out my story more completely. As with most theological shifts and changes in my life, my change about infant baptism was a long, slow process. I gradually realized, as a result of Bible studies on specific issues and readings with major theologians and conversations with friends, that I believed in infant baptism. As I said, it was a process, and this is a basic sketch of how I changed my mind.

Before getting there I must say two things. The first is this: those of us who believe in infant baptism bear some responsibility for the horrendous persecution unleashed on those who became "Baptist" or "Anabaptist"—that is, those who believed infant baptism was not biblical and who believed adult or believer's baptism was biblical and *who were persecuted, many to death, for that choice*. The history of the Anabaptists at the heavy deathly hand of Roman Catholics, Lutherans, and the Reformed of Switzerland and beyond is ugly, embarrassing, and something that bothers me to this day. One of my all-time favorite Anabaptists, Michael Sattler, was hideously persecuted: his tongue was cut off, and he was chained to a cart and tortured with hot tongs before he was burned to death.[1] To them I apologize and confess that those of us who believe in infant baptism were wrong, sorrowfully wrong, for behavior that was not only uncivil but profoundly wrong for any Christian.[2]

The second is like the first: I express my respect for many evangelical Christians today who were nurtured in an infant-baptism church context but who later, and often under some pressure from teachers, pastors, family members, and friends exhorting believer's baptism, were rebaptized by immersion. (Not a few I know have not only walked a journey from infant to believer's baptism but are now backing up into churches that baptize infants because they have reconsidered infant baptism and come to affirm it.) Most importantly, some of those who walked away from their infant baptism into believer's baptism suffered shame and family tension because of that move. That experience is worthy of our respect, even if we think the path taken was (as I now believe) mistaken. But it is also fair to come back and say that when someone chooses to be rebaptized, they do so believing that the original baptism actually accomplished nothing, that it was in effect merely a symbolic (and nonsacramental) action. They may well also be saying that baptism is more about what *they do* (or believe) than what *God does*. But what if we join the heritage of the church and affirm with the Anglicans that baptism *as an act in the church* is sacramental and never merely symbolic? If we were to do this, we would be wise to rethink the decision to be rebaptized.

I came to faith in the kind of Baptist environment described above, which meant baptism was for us a symbolic act of my own faith in Christ. It was for believers only, and it was often about the faith of the believer. As such, and this is not disparaging, the act of baptism itself *accomplished* nothing. It dramatized and witnessed to our personal faith in Christ. No one in my church was permitted to be baptized until he or she could offer a credible testimony of personal reception of Christ. This happened for me when I was about six years old. I had gotten on my knees with my mother and asked Christ to come into my heart. A few years later I went through a question-and-answer form of instruction, and then I was interviewed by a deacon. Upon his recommendation to the deacon board, I was permitted to be baptized. My baptism occurred on a hot summer evening at First Baptist Church in Freeport, Illinois. As I recall it, I was far more nervous about having to give my brief testimony to my pastor in front of a few hundred people than I was cognizant of this being a profound transition in my faith. But it was both.

I have never questioned my faith, but I have had questions aplenty about what the Bible teaches and what the church tradition has taught about baptism. My first serious questioning came early in my seminary education when I decided to investigate the texts and literature to determine once and for all what I believed. Little did I know that "once and for all" rarely happens for those who live a life among theologians, because if we don't grow we stagnate. Previously, while in college in Grand Rapids, I had encountered constant conversations about infant baptism because of the abundance—"overabundance" might be the better word—of Dutch Reformed Calvinists who baptized their babies. So in seminary I decided one summer to make this my subject of study. I read some major books on both sides, including the Baptist George Beasley-Murray and the Anglican Geoffrey Bromiley.[3] At the time, I thought the Baptist Beasley-Murray had the better arguments as Bromiley didn't have enough Bible for my own approach to forming our beliefs. Some of Bromiley's arguments, however, stuck with me for good. I took a course in seminary—an advanced course in Greek exegesis and grammar—that investigated baptism texts in the New Testament. I enjoyed the course with a number of close friends, and we had a good teacher, but I don't recall that the course did anything but confirm my Baptist conclusions.

Over the years of teaching in one college and two seminaries, both of which seminaries were and are baptistic in stance but generous in their orthodoxy so that both sides of the spectrum have been embraced, I was teaching the Bible and reading books and engaging the conversation. All during that time I constantly encountered pastors, theologians, and lay folks who were baptized as infants who embraced that view and at times spoke of living out their baptism. Some of my best Christian students at North Park University were baptized as infants. Many of my favorite theologians and pastors, from Dietrich Bonhoeffer to John Stott to Alexander Schmemann to N. T. Wright, believe in infant baptism. But their own support did not shift my mind. What shifted my mind was the Bible (as I understand it).

First, the connection of covenant and circumcision to covenant and baptism in Colossians 2:11–12 forced me to think harder about circumcision and its relationship to infant baptism. What shook my Baptist beliefs was that Abraham's circumcision was tied to his faith but that he circumcised his son Isaac without one word about Isaac's faith. What is more, God told Israelites to circumcise their boys on the eighth day, which means we have to think that children were incorporated into the faith of their parents *by divine decree*. That God was behind the covenant circumcision of eight-day-olds penetrated deeply into my heart. I have therefore emphasized in this book God's order to circumcise infants of covenanted Israelites and thus to incorporate them into the covenant-faith family.

A second shift in my understanding convinced me even more. Much is said about household baptisms in the early church, but the singular biblical consideration for me was that it was socially and historically nearly impossible for there to have been no children or infants in each of those homes mentioned in the Bible. What is more, when a parent (father) of that time turned from the world to Christ and believed, his baptism was extended to everyone in the home. I saw in this a reflection of the very principle of covenant circumcision: the faith of the believing adult is expanded to include the children. Another emphasis of my shifting of conclusions is that in the ancient world, including Judaism and therefore earliest Christianity, a person's faith was far more often inherited than chosen. To have baptized an infant would have been seen as nothing but commonplace. On top of this I could explain 1 Corinthians 7:14's description of children becoming "holy" on the basis of a parent's faith. I was convinced that infant baptism was at work already in the era of the apostles. In the end, I do believe that we must make a choice on what is uppermost about baptism: Is baptism something we do or something God does?

Two arguments from silence have also confirmed my conviction that the early church did in fact baptize infants. The first comes from the tried and true practices of Judaism: (1) Judaism from the time of its inception practiced the incorporation of children into the faith. (2) Jesus and the apostles grew up in the kind of culture that immediately incorporated children into one's faith. (3) There is no record that Jesus or the apostles opposed the incorporation of children into the faith of the church. Why? They thought this was the way things ought to be done. Their silence is an eloquent support of infant baptism.

The second argument from silence is the story that, since the earliest days of Christianity, only professing adults were baptized but that in the second or third centuries infant baptism began to be practiced. The problems with this story is what it lacks: if there was a change from adult to infant baptism, why is there no record that there was a sudden or even comprehensive shift, or any evidence of early Christian theologians holding up a red flag to say, "Hey, we are departing from the tried and true practice of the apostles"? Again, that silence has a similar eloquence.

These arguments then pushed me to reframe baptism into a covenant and family context for spiritual formation. Baptism, it must be emphasized, launches that person into the covenant of redemption. I like—with one quibble—how Michael Green summarizes baptism's meaning:

> It is the rite of entry into the Christian church. It is ineffective [for full redemption][4] until there is repentance and faith, but it stresses the initiative of God. It offers to us all the blessings of the covenant between God's grace and our response. It binds us into a unity of life not only with Jesus Christ but with all baptized believers the world over. And it plunges us into that most profound of mysteries, the dying and rising of Jesus Christ our Lord.[5]

The Evangelical Challenge

Yet, convinced as I am of the biblical basis for infant baptism, I have too much evangelicalism in my soul to close the curtains on this book without emphasizing the necessity of personal faith. An evangelical is someone who believes in the priority of Scripture, the cruciality of the cross as God's means of redemption, the necessity of personal faith and conversion, and the implication of living out that faith in evangelism and good works. Furthermore, evangelicalism stretches beyond denominational borders.[6] I believe all these things to the core of my being.

Which leaves me with this issue: How can one baptize an infant, drawing such a person into the church, and maintain the necessity of personal faith? To answer this question I want to turn to one who has always been known for his evangelical faith and who has looked at this very problem himself: John Stott, a well-known evangelical Anglican. Stott on more than one topic has changed my mind. What he says about infant baptism corresponds to *It Takes a Church to Baptize*, though I'd slightly rephrase some of what he says. First, he looks at what baptism is, and on this we agree:

> Baptism is therefore to be understood as an eschatological sacrament, inasmuch as it initiates into the New Covenant which belongs to the New Age. It does this by incorporating us *into Christ*, for Jesus Christ is the mediator of the New Covenant, and the bestower of its blessings.

I like this way of expressing it and would only suggest bringing the church into it a little more. Stott then turns to the theology of baptism:

> To sum up, baptism signifies union with Jesus Christ in his death and resurrection, involving the end of the old life (through the forgiveness of sins) and the beginning of a new life (through the gift of the Spirit). Alternatively, baptism signifies union with Christ bringing both justification (a once for all cleansing and acceptance) and regeneration (a new birth by the Spirit unto a life of righteousness). To these three meanings of baptism we

must add that incorporation into Christ includes incorporation into the Body of Christ, the Church.[7]

Stott's emphasis on the term "incorporation" is very important: baptism incorporates the baptized into Christ and into the body of Christ—that is, the church. This term also emphasizes baptism as something done to us in God's grace, not something we do.

Stott goes on to look at texts such as 1 Corinthians 7:14 and Colossians 2:11–12, observing that "baptism does not convey these blessings to us, but conveys to us a right or title to them, so that if and when we truly believe, we inherit the blessings to which baptism has entitled us."[8] I believe Stott is weakening what he has said with the term "incorporation." If baptism incorporates us, then baptism actually does accomplish something. It incorporates that child into the journey of faith in Christ. But Stott knows that baptism for believing adults and baptism for infants surrounded by family and the church are not the same, and in this he is right:

> To *truly believing adults* the covenant sign of baptism (like circumcision to Abraham when he was ninety-nine years old) signifies and seals a grace which has already been received by faith [for the believing adult]. To *the infant seed* of believing parents, the covenant sign of baptism (like circumcision to Isaac at the age of eight days) is administered because they are born into the covenant and are thereby "holy" in which they still need to receive later by faith.[9]

Seeds are nonetheless seeds, and seeds need to be watered so they will grow. But Stott, ever the evangelist and ever concerned that we not think faith is automatic for our children and ever urging us to evangelize from the family out, makes an important turn toward the necessity of personal faith as the baptized infant grows into adulthood:

> People need to be warned, for the good of their soul, that the reception of the sign, although it entitles them to the gift, does not confer the gift on them. *They need to be taught the indispensable necessity of personal repentance and faith if they are to receive the thing signified.*[10]

When he says "they need to be taught" I concur wholeheartedly, and the biblical context for that teaching is a covenant-based family and a covenant-based church all attending to the formation of its youth from birth and baptism into adulthood. Baptism as an act *does accomplish something*, but baptism unattended by personal faith *doesn't accomplish its full design*. To be faithful to the God of the Bible, who brought infants into the covenant with Israel and with Christ, we need to plant the seed of grace in the infant and exhort that child to believe, to obey, and to live in the grace of baptism.

Criticisms of infant baptism that fail to consider the important role of families in the formation of faith are hollow criticisms, just as defenses of infant baptism without emphasizing the important role of parents in the context of a church are hollow. Infant baptism, I have come to believe, is embedded in how one understands the church and the family as integral institutions of formation. The more individualistic one makes faith, the less likely it is that one will see the family-covenant connection of circumcision and baptism. The crudest example of this is self-baptism. However, the more one emphasizes baptism as an act of God in the context of a church- and family-based faith formation, the more one will embrace infant baptism as most consistent with the Bible's vision.

Afterword

Some decades ago I was a Baptist pastor. Then one day I was reading the New Testament and became disturbed by passages that I had read perhaps a hundred times before but that suddenly took on new meaning. The first was 1 Corinthians 10:16, which made me rethink my presumption that the Lord's Supper was merely a mental remembrance of what happened two thousand years ago. Then it was a pair of passages (Rom. 6 and Col. 2) that made me reconsider baptism. While reading the first few verses of the Romans passage it suddenly dawned on me that baptism was here described not as something that *we* do, but as something that *God* does to us. In baptism, Paul writes, we were "baptized *into* Christ" and "*into* his death" (6:3). We were "buried with him through baptism into death" (v. 4) and somehow "*united* with him" (v. 5). In some mysterious way, baptism for Paul is an event in which "our old self was crucified with him" (v. 6).

For some years I had believed and preached that baptism is merely something *we* do to proclaim to the world that we are disciples of Jesus. I had assumed that there was nothing mysterious or supernatural going on when we were immersed or sprinkled with water. We were merely obeying what Scripture tells us to do.

Then Colossians 2 struck with equal force. There (vv. 11–12) baptism is compared to Jewish circumcision. I knew that in circumcision a little Jewish boy was brought into God's covenant with Israel. This was not mere symbolism but a real event in the history of redemption, so that this little boy was forever changed. The rabbis and his parents now considered him to be a "son of the covenant" in a way that marked him forever. So baptism, the author of Colossians tells us, is the New Testament equivalent of circumcision. It is a "circumcision not performed by human hands" when "the flesh was put off," "having been buried with [Christ] in baptism."

Then I saw other scriptures about baptism that I had previously overlooked. Jesus said we must be born again "of *water* and the Spirit" (John 3:5), as if somehow the water conveys the Spirit. In his letter to Titus, Paul links water to regeneration: "He saved us . . . through the *water* of rebirth and renewal by the Holy Spirit" (3:5 NRSV).

Again, it seemed, baptism is not what *we* do but something that *God* does *to* us. Baptism unites us with the God of Israel's Son, the Messiah Jesus. Because of this, since he died and rose again, we died and rose with him. Faith is necessary to keep us united with him, but in baptism a mysterious work of God by the Spirit begins.

My Baptist predilections at first resisted these discoveries. Did this mean that baptism automatically saves? I knew far too many skeptics and profligates who had been baptized as infants. Then I came to realize, slowly, that while baptism confers something real, it can be neglected, with eternal consequences. Later I came to liken it to what happens to a newborn child whose parent signs over the estate to the child, provided that the child claim it upon maturity. It has often happened that children in that situation grow up to hate their parents. They refuse the estate and forfeit their inheritance. That is what happens to all those who turn away from God and the gift he gave them in baptism.

In grad school I started reading the fathers of the early church. Shortly after my own discoveries of Romans 6 and Colossians 2, I discovered that the fathers had a similar view of baptism. Justin Martyr wrote that in Rome the baptized are "brought by us [to] where there is water, and are reborn by the same manner of rebirth by which we ourselves were reborn" (*First Apology* 61). Tertullian wrote that "the waters have in some sense acquired [by prayer] healing power . . . [so that] the spirit [of the baptized] is in those waters corporally washed, while the flesh is in those same waters spiritually cleansed" (*Baptism* 4). The *Apostolic Tradition* has the bishop pray, "You have made them worthy to receive remission of sins through the laver of regeneration of the Holy Spirit" (21). Sarapion, bishop of Thmuis in northern Egypt, spoke of the baptized who were "purified through the *bath* and renewed in the Spirit" (*Prayers* 15). Irenaeus links baptism to the forgiveness of sins (*Demonstration of the Apostolic Preaching* 3).

But what about the baptism of infants? As my friend Scot has shown, there is evidence that this was the near-universal practice of the church for its first fifteen centuries. As the great Augustine put it, "Whether it be a newborn infant or a decrepit old man— since no one should be barred from baptism—just so, there is no one who does not die to sin in baptism" (*Enchiridion* 43).

Once I recognized the link between Old Testament circumcision and New Testament baptism, the inclusion of infants was something of a no-brainer. After all, Paul wrote that circumcision was the seal of the covenant that was the sign of the righteousness that comes by faith (Rom. 4:11). While circumcision came after faith for Abraham, it came *before* faith for Isaac. So Paul apparently had no problem reconciling faith as necessary for salvation, on the one hand, and circumcision for babies without evident signs of conscious faith, on the other.

But there is further New Testament evidence, if not proof. Throughout the Bible, God deals with families: Abraham, Noah, the jailer at Philippi. Scot has detailed some of this evidence in this book. He has also discussed Paul's statement about the children of believers: "your children . . . are holy" (1 Cor. 7:14). This was not moral holiness or civil legitimacy but covenant status. When God brings families into his covenant, he consecrates their children. It seemed particularly appropriate for Jewish believers to baptize their infants since they were used to circumcising their infant sons and to believing that circumcision bestowed this new status on those sons.

Scot has discussed the New Testament household salvations—of the families of Lydia, the jailer at Philippi, Stephanas, and probably Cornelius. There is no explicit mention of infants in these household baptisms, but it is likely since the early church leaders were Jews who probably took baptism from the practice of first-century Jews such as John the Baptist. But there is another intriguing source. We have good historical evidence that when gentiles converted to Judaism, their whole households—which often included children and infants—were baptized. Most Jewish leaders undoubtedly knew about these household baptisms.

For many years I said that I became a Christian when I had a conscious conversion to Jesus at the age of eighteen. But now I am not so sure. Now I think of my infant baptism and of the fear of God it seems to have instilled in me for my first eighteen years. Although I committed some serious sins, this fear kept me from others that would have wrecked my life. It also helped me understand what Jonathan Edwards meant when he explained that regeneration can come years before conscious conversion to Jesus. Both he and John Calvin believed that Cornelius, for example, was already regenerate before he heard Peter tell him about Jesus. For Edwards, Cornelius might have been regenerate for years before he found the Jewish Messiah.

Now I tell people that I believe the Holy Spirit planted a seed in me at my infant baptism, a seed that finally bore fruit in conversion eighteen years later.

Gerald R. McDermott
Anglican Chair of Divinity
Beeson Divinity School

Notes

Preface

1. Letter to author, January 30, 2017. Used with permission.

2. Michael Green, *Baptism: Its Purpose, Practice, and Power* (Downers Grove, IL: InterVarsity, 1987), 63–64.

Chapter 1: Our Baptism

1. There is a growing concern among Baptists to invest more theology in adult or believer's baptism, and I'm grateful for their serious efforts. One book stands out as an early example: George R. Beasley-Murray, *Baptism in the New Testament* (Grand Rapids: Eerdmans, 1962). A collection of more recent essays by various Baptist scholars is too polemical and ignores the Anglican, Orthodox, and Catholic variations on infant baptism; see Thomas R. Schreiner and Shawn D. Wright, eds., *Believer's Baptism: Sign of the New Covenant in Christ* (Nashville: B&H, 2007). Timothy George's foreword to the Schreiner and Wright volume complements what I will say in this book. George thinks Baptists need to renew the essential practices of baptism by (1) making it a central element of Christian worship, (2) shaping it by discipleship commitments, and (3) forming it by a theology of children. I wish the rest of the chapters in the Schreiner and Wright volume had incorporated the insights and civility of George.

2. Dietrich Bonhoeffer, *Discipleship*, Dietrich Bonhoeffer Works 4 (Minneapolis: Fortress, 2001), 211–12 (italics mine).

3. Bryan Chapell, *Why Do We Baptize Infants? Basics of the Faith* (Phillipsburg, NJ: P&R, 2006), 15. Here are his arguments: (1) the argument from silence—that is, that there is no contrary command in a world where something performed on infants would be the Jewish custom, and (2) household

baptism implies children and others (15–24). Neither proves; each is, however, at least suggestive.

4. However, it should be observed that the word "hinder" in Mark 10:14, since it is found in baptismal contexts in Acts 8:36; 10:47; and 11:17, is taken by some to refer already in the first century to a debate about infant baptism; see Oscar Cullmann, *Baptism in the New Testament*, trans. J. K. S. Reid, Studies in Biblical Theology 1 (London: SCM, 1950), 71–80; Joachim Jeremias, *Infant Baptism in the First Four Centuries*, trans. D. Cairns (London: SCM, 1960), 51–55. Their theory is challenged by the ecclesial traditions of the early church by David F. Wright, "Out, In, Out: Jesus' Blessing of the Children and Infant Baptism," in *Dimensions of Baptism: Biblical and Theological Studies*, ed. Stanley Porter and Anthony R. Cross, Journal for the Study of the New Testament 234 (London: Sheffield Academic, 2002), 188–206.

5. But notice that the mode of baptism varies, and this from Didache 7.1–4: "But with respect to baptism, baptize as follows. Having said all these things in advance, baptize in the name of the Father and of the Son and of the Holy Spirit, in running water. But if you do not have running water, baptize in some other water. And if you cannot baptize in cold water, use warm. But if you have neither, pour water on the head three times in the name of Father and Son and Holy Spirit. But both the one baptizing and the one being baptized should fast before the baptism, along with some others if they can. But command the one being baptized to fast one or two days in advance."

6. Roger W. Gehring, *House Church and Mission: The Importance of Household Structures in Early Christianity* (Peabody, MA: Hendrickson, 2004); Peter Oakes, *Reading Romans in Pompeii: Paul's Letter at Ground Level* (Minneapolis: Fortress, 2009). It is surely probable that some households had no infants, but it is highly unlikely that each of the household conversions and baptisms in the texts above had no infants or children. Witherington's discussion that concludes there is no evidence for infants in the households is unconvincing because the word "household" *means and includes* infants and children—that is, if they are present; see Ben Witherington III, *Troubled Waters: The Real New Theology of Baptism* (Waco: Baylor University Press, 2007), 59–68. The least we can infer from these texts is that *we don't know whether there were infants* or that *there may have been infants*. To argue their absence from their not being mentioned contradicts the meaning of "household."

7. These verses need to be backed up with Exod. 12:43–49; Num. 9:6–14; and Isa. 35:8; 52:1.

8. The routine presence of ritual ablutions for crossing life's thresholds makes *some kind of ritual* almost necessary for first-century folks, especially Jewish folks. On this, see Mary Douglas, *Purity and Danger: An Analysis of Concepts of Pollution and Taboo* (New York: Routledge, 2002); Catherine

Bell, *Ritual Theory, Ritual Practice* (New York: Oxford University Press, 2009); Catherine Bell, *Ritual: Perspectives and Dimensions*, rev. ed. (New York: Oxford University Press, 2009); Gerard S. Sloyan, "Jewish Ritual of the First Century C.E. and Christian Sacramental Behavior," *Biblical Theology Bulletin* 15, no. 3 (1985): 98–103. The implication for anything done to children lies close at hand. A timely expression from baptism's most exhaustive study: "Only a few (fringe) heretics of the ancient church tried to dehydrate the new birth." Everett Ferguson, *Baptism in the Early Church: History, Theology, and Liturgy in the First Five Centuries* (Grand Rapids: Eerdmans, 2009), 854.

9. Throughout this book I will often cite the Bible verses I am using, but in this first chapter I want to include the text of the verses I'm referring to in hopes that the reader will examine them closely.

10. Scot McKnight, *The King Jesus Gospel: The Original Good News Revisited*, 2nd ed. (Grand Rapids: Zondervan, 2015).

11. Matthew W. Bates, *Salvation by Allegiance Alone: Rethinking Faith, Works, and the Gospel of Jesus the King* (Grand Rapids: Baker Academic, 2017).

12. Scot McKnight, *Turning to Jesus: The Sociology of Conversion in the Gospels* (Louisville: Westminster John Knox, 2002).

13. This same set of observations can be made about the conversion of Mary.

14. I write about this in McKnight, *Turning to Jesus*, 1–25.

15. *The Book of Common Prayer: According to the Use of the Episcopal Church* (New York: Oxford University Press, 1990), 872. I am aware that some prefer older versions of *The Book of Common Prayer* and that the Anglican Church of North America is freshly preparing its own version. I use the Episcopal Church version because of its accessibility. An alternative baptism liturgy, often used in our baptismal services at Church of the Redeemer, can be found in *Common Worship* and is available at https://www .churchofengland.org/prayer-worship/worship/texts/christian-initiation /baptism-and-confirmation/holy-baptism.aspx.

16. *Book of Common Prayer*, 873.

17. Karl Barth, *Church Dogmatics* IV/4 (frag.), *The Foundation of the Christian Life: Baptism*, trans. Geoffrey W. Bromiley and T. F. Torrance, study ed. (London: T&T Clark, 2009), 165.

18. Donald Bridge and David Phypers, *The Water That Divides: The Baptism Debate* (Downers Grove, IL: InterVarsity, 2008); David F. Wright, ed., *Baptism: Three Views* (Downers Grove, IL: IVP Academic, 2009); John H. Armstrong, ed., *Understanding Four Views on Baptism* (Grand Rapids: Zondervan, 2007).

19. Restorationists are Churches of Christ, Christian Churches, and Disciples of Christ. There are, however, some significant differences among

Restorationists. A major view of this group can be found in Ferguson, *Baptism in the Early Church*.

20. For the Orthodox view, see Alexander Schmemann, *Of Water and the Spirit: A Liturgical Study of Baptism* (Crestwood, NY: St. Vladimir's Seminary Press, 1997). For the Catholic view, the principal beliefs can be found in the Catechism of the Catholic Church at http://www.vatican.va /archive/ccc_css/archive/catechism/p2s2c1a1.htm.

21. For a history of the Anabaptists, I recommend William R. Estep, *The Anabaptist Story: An Introduction to Sixteenth-Century Anabaptism*, 3rd ed. (Grand Rapids: Eerdmans, 1996).

22. *Book of Common Prayer*, 873.

23. Dietrich Bonhoeffer, "A Theological Position Paper on the Question of Baptism," in *Conspiracy and Imprisonment, 1940–1945*, ed. Mark S. Brocker, trans. Lisa F. Dahill, Dietrich Bonhoeffer Works 16 (Minneapolis: Fortress, 2006), 551–72.

24. Bonhoeffer, "Question of Baptism," 551.

25. For a solid, if dense, description of baptism in the early church, see Andrew B. McGowan, *Ancient Christian Worship: Early Church Practices in Social, Historical, and Theological Perspective* (Grand Rapids: Baker Academic, 2014), 135–75.

26. This set of quotations was collected by Ethan McCarthy and passed on to me. I have cited a few of these in other locations throughout the book. A fuller listing can be found at http://www.churchfathers.org/category/sacra ments/infant-baptism.

27. Translation from Everett Ferguson's revision of Thomas Scheck's translation; Ferguson, "Baptism according to Origen," *Evangelical Quarterly* 78 (2006): 130.

28. To be sure, not a few of the church's theologians believed in baptismal forgiveness; that is, infants needed baptism due to original sin and therefore were condemned until baptism. For discussion of this view, see Ferguson, *Baptism in the Early Church*, 378–79. This belief in original sin, guilt, and condemnation—and in the power of infant baptism to undo that guilt—is no small source of serious disagreement among Baptist critics of infant baptism.

Chapter 2: Baptism

1. For a larger-than-life biography of the larger-than-life Cranmer, see Diarmaid MacCulloch, *Thomas Cranmer: A Life* (New Haven: Yale University Press, 1996). For a study of *The Book of Common Prayer*, see Alan Jacobs, *The "Book of Common Prayer": A Biography*, Lives of Great Religious Books (Princeton and Oxford: Princeton University Press, 2013).

2. At Church of the Redeemer our pastor, Jay Greener, now uses *Common Worship*, and I will at times observe some differences between *The Book of*

Common Prayer: According to the Use of the Episcopal Church (New York: Oxford University Press, 1990), 299–314, and *Common Worship*.

3. *Common Worship* begins with words that emphasize the theology of baptism, which we will discuss in a later chapter: "Our Lord Jesus Christ has told us that to enter the kingdom of heaven we must be born again of water and the Spirit, and has given us baptism as the sign and seal of this new birth. Here we are washed by the Holy Spirit and made clean. Here we are clothed with Christ, dying to sin that we may live his risen life. As children of God, we have a new dignity and God calls us to fullness of life."

4. Of course some of the baptisms of John the Baptist were in public and were in the Jordan River and not in the context of the church, but the church had not yet been formed. Baptisms get connected to churches about as quickly as churches were formed.

5. Two studies can be mentioned here: Robert N. Bellah, Richard Madsen, William M. Sullivan, Ann Swidler, and Steven M, Tipton, *Habits of the Heart: Individualism and Commitment in American Life* (New York: Harper & Row, 1985); and Robert D. Putnam, *Bowling Alone: The Collapse and Revival of American Community* (New York: Simon & Schuster, 2000).

6. Again, I mention two studies: Kenda Creasy Dean, *Almost Christian: What the Faith of Our Teenagers Is Telling the American Church* (New York: Oxford University Press, 2010); and Kara E. Powell and Chap Clark, *Sticky Faith: Everyday Ideas to Build Lasting Faith in Your Kids* (Grand Rapids: Zondervan, 2011). The most important analysis of church and youth has been carried out by Christian Smith and associates: Christian Smith and Melinda Lundquist Denton, *Soul Searching: The Religious and Spiritual Lives of American Teenagers* (New York: Oxford University Press, 2009); Christian Smith and Patricia Snell, *Souls in Transition: The Religious and Spiritual Lives of Emerging Adults* (New York: Oxford University Press, 2009); and Christian Smith with Kari Christoffersen, Hilary Davidson, and Patricia Snell Herzog, *Lost in Transition: The Dark Side of Emerging Adulthood* (New York: Oxford University Press, 2011).

7. The scenario that entails immigration and later citizenship can be set aside for the moment.

8. Marilynne Robinson, *Gilead* (New York: Farrar, Straus and Giroux, 2004). This quote and those that follow are drawn from pp. 24–26.

9. Harper Lee, *Go Set a Watchman: A Novel* (New York: Harper, 2015), 64–67.

Chapter 3: Presentation and Commitments

1. Sponsors arose because of persecution. A person might approach for baptism only to infiltrate the Christian church, discover who participates, and then turn those names into authorities for persecution. A sponsor was a trustworthy witness for the candidate.

2. J. I. Packer, *Baptism and Regeneration* (Newport Beach, CA: Anglican House, 2014), 8–9.

3. I wrote about this in *The Jesus Creed: Loving God, Loving Others*, 10th anniv. ed. (Brewster, MA: Paraclete, 2014).

4. Kara E. Powell and Chap Clark, *Sticky Faith: Everyday Ideas to Build Lasting Faith in Your Kids* (Grand Rapids: Zondervan, 2011).

5. Michael Green, *Baptism: Its Purpose, Practice, and Power* (Downers Grove, IL: InterVarsity, 1987), 96–97.

6. In *Common Worship* two other features precede the confession of the creed: making the sign of the cross on the forehead of each person being baptized and praying over the water. We will encounter these themes later in *The Book of Common Prayer* (see chap. 6 below).

7. If you want to read more about the Nicene or Apostles' Creed, I recommend Alister McGrath, *"I Believe": Exploring the Apostles' Creed* (Downers Grove, IL: InterVarsity, 1998). I also recommend the Ancient Christian Doctrine series by InterVarsity Press for a more academic discussion.

8. Not present in *Common Worship*, but similar instructions are found in the commission near the end of Holy Baptism.

9. Alexander Schmemann, *Of Water and the Spirit: A Liturgical Study of Baptism* (Crestwood, NY: St. Vladimir's Seminary Press, 1997), 66–70.

Chapter 4: The Three Great Themes of Our Baptism

1. *The Book of Common Prayer: According to the Use of the Episcopal Church* (New York: Oxford University Press, 1990), 868.

2. In chapter 2 I used the terms "theology" and "big ideas" for what I believe is "capable of proof from the Bible."

3. I have a discussion of the problem at Colossae in Scot McKnight, *The Letter to Colossians*, NICNT (Grand Rapids: Eerdmans, 2018).

4. For a more complete discussion, see McKnight, *The Jesus Creed: Loving God, Loving Others*, 10th anniv. ed. (Brewster, MA: Paraclete, 2014), 65–74.

5. James D. G. Dunn, *Baptism in the Holy Spirit: A Re-Examination of the New Testament Teaching on the Gift of the Holy Spirit in Relation to Pentecostalism Today* (Philadelphia: Westminster, 1970); Dunn, *Beginning from Jerusalem*, Christianity in the Making 2 (Grand Rapids: Eerdmans, 2009), 185–89, 649–52; Ben Witherington III, *Troubled Waters: The Real New Theology of Baptism* (Waco: Baylor University Press, 2007). The debate following Dunn's claim (that one receives the Spirit at the moment of faith and initiation into relation with Christ, not as a subsequent experience) finds its charismatic alternative in William P. Atkinson, *Baptism in the Spirit: Luke-Acts and the Dunn Debate* (Eugene, OR: Wipf & Stock, 2011). I am grateful to Tom Lyons, a PhD student at Asbury Theological Seminary, for pointing me to this study by Atkinson.

6. For discussion, Robin M. Jensen, *Baptismal Imagery in Early Christianity: Ritual, Visual, and Theological Dimensions* (Grand Rapids: Baker Academic, 2012), 94–115.

7. Anthony R. Cross, "Spirit- and Water-Baptism in 1 Corinthians 12.13," in *Dimensions of Baptism: Biblical and Theological Studies*, ed. Stanley Porter and Anthony R. Cross, Journal for the Study of the New Testament 234 (London: Sheffield Academic, 2002), 120–48.

8. Dietrich Bonhoeffer, "A Theological Position Paper on the Question of Baptism," in *Conspiracy and Imprisonment, 1940–1945*, ed. Mark S. Brocker, trans. Lisa F. Dahill, Dietrich Bonhoeffer Works 16 (Minneapolis: Fortress, 2006), 556.

9. Kevin J. Vanhoozer, *Biblical Authority after Babel: Retrieving the Solas in the Spirit of Mere Protestant Christianity* (Grand Rapids: Brazos, 2016).

10. Article 25, *Book of Common Prayer*, 872.

11. *Book of Common Prayer*, 857.

12. Michael Green, *Baptism: Its Purpose, Practice, and Power* (Downers Grove, IL: InterVarsity, 1987), 56.

13. Lars Hartman, *"Into the Name of Jesus": Baptism in the Early Church*, Studies of the New Testament and Its World (Edinburgh: T&T Clark, 1997), 168.

14. Richard Pratt Jr., "Reformed View: Baptism as a Sacrament of the Covenant," in *Understanding Four Views on Baptism*, ed. John H. Armstrong (Grand Rapids: Zondervan, 2007), 59.

15. Carl R. Trueman, *Grace Alone—Salvation as a Gift of God: What the Reformers Taught . . . and Why It Still Matters* (Grand Rapids: Zondervan, 2017), 197. He is right that the biggest difference is not over *who is to be baptized* (infants or confessing adults) but over *who is most responsible in baptism* (God or the human responding in faith); see 204–7.

Chapter 5: The Bible and Infant Baptism

1. One of the great debates about baptism occurred two generations ago between two Germans, one a Lutheran and the other a Baptist: see Joachim Jeremias, *Infant Baptism in the First Four Centuries*, trans. D. Cairns (London: SCM, 1960); Kurt Aland, *Did the Early Church Baptize Infants?*, trans. George R. Beasley-Murray (London: SCM, 1963); Joachim Jeremias, *The Origins of Infant Baptism: A Further Study in Reply to Kurt Aland*, trans. Dorothea M. Barton, Studies in Historical Theology 1 (London: SCM, 1963). On household baptisms, see Jeremias, *Origins*, 12–32; Ben Witherington III, *Troubled Waters: The Real New Theology of Baptism* (Waco: Baylor University Press, 2007), 59–68; Daniel R. Hyde, *Jesus Loves the Little Children: Why We Baptize Children* (Grandville, MI: Reformed Fellowship, 2012), 43–46. Everett Ferguson draws the opposite conclusion; namely, the *absence* of children in accounts where an author otherwise mentions women (Acts

5:14; 8:12) indicates they were not part of household baptisms; see Ferguson, *Baptism in the Early Church: History, Theology, and Liturgy in the First Five Centuries* (Grand Rapids: Eerdmans, 2009), 185. For a good survey of the arguments for household baptisms/conversions implying infant baptism, with which he then disagrees, see George R. Beasley-Murray, *Baptism in the New Testament* (Grand Rapids: Eerdmans, 1962), 312–20.

For a powerful display of the revolutionary nature of household baptisms relocating the household as a new culture and spiritual center, see esp. J. B. Green, "'She and Her Household Were Baptized' (Acts 16.15): Household Baptism in the Acts of the Apostles," in *Dimensions of Baptism: Biblical and Theological Studies*, ed. Stanley Porter and Anthony R. Cross, Journal for the Study of the New Testament 234 (London: Sheffield Academic, 2002), 72–90. His conclusion: "The baptism of households entails the unequivocal embrace of the household as the new culture center for the people of God, an active center of social order that embodies and radiates a world-order within which Jesus is Lord of all, hospitality is shared across socio-ethnic lines, and hierarchical lines that define the empire are erased" (90).

2. For an extraordinary study of what a household actually comprised in the first century (in Pompeii), see Peter Oakes, *Reading Romans in Pompeii: Paul's Letter at Ground Level* (Minneapolis: Fortress, 2009).

3. Again, see Oakes, *Reading Romans*.

4. With these texts clearly now on the table, I must say that the Baptist defender of adult baptism is clearly mistaken in the following claim: "Every New Testament instruction or command regarding baptism, and every clear instance of baptism that we see in the New Testament, relates to the baptism of those who have repented of sin (John's baptism) and come to faith in Christ (baptisms from Pentecost forward)." Bruce Ware, "Believers' Baptism View," in Sinclair B. Ferguson, Bruce A. Ware, and Anthony N. S. Lane, *Baptism: Three Views*, ed. David F. Wright (Downers Grove, IL: IVP Academic, 2009), 23.

5. The following is drawn from Hippolytus, *Apostolic Tradition* 21.1–5.

6. For discussions of this in the early churches, see Robin M. Jensen, *Baptismal Imagery in Early Christianity: Ritual, Visual, and Theological Dimensions* (Grand Rapids: Baker Academic, 2012), 167–72.

7. For a sketch of the evidence in the early church, especially with respect to anointing the whole body with oil, see Jensen, *Baptismal Imagery*, 40–42.

8. To read an imaginative retelling of an early Christian baptism, see Martin E. Marty, *Baptism* (Philadelphia: Fortress, 1962), 4–5.

9. Thanks to Ethan McCarthy for this point.

10. This early liturgy for baptism then proceeds to the commitments already discussed, including one of the earliest versions of the Apostles' Creed, followed by chrismation, a pastoral prayer, and the passing of the peace. Baptism naturally then led to the Eucharist, or "first communion."

11. Jeremias, *Origins*, 24.

12. J. I. Packer, *Baptism and Regeneration* (Newport Beach, CA: Anglican House, 2014), 7.

13. The history of the liturgy of baptism—what was confessed, what was done (who baptized, triple baptism in trinitarian fashion, nudity for the baptisand, laying on of hands, anointing, robing, renunciation of Satan, Eucharist, catechumenate, etc.) and the order of any kind of baptismal "service"—is beyond the scope of this book. See the sketch of scholarship in Ferguson, *Baptism in the Early Church*, 5–11. On imagery for baptism and a full display of early Christian practice, see Jensen, *Baptismal Imagery*.

14. Oscar Cullmann, *Baptism in the New Testament*, trans. J. K. S. Reid, Studies in Biblical Theology 1 (London: SCM, 1950), 50.

15. To be more precise, Abram's name was not changed until Gen. 17:5 to "Abraham." I will use "Abraham" throughout.

16. On circumcision I mention only two standard treatments, each of which gives the pertinent information: L. A. Hoffman, "Circumcision," in *Encyclopedia of Judaism*, ed. Jacob Neusner, Alan J. Avery-Peck, and William Scott Green (New York: Continuum, 1999), 1:89–95; D. A. Bernat, "Circumcision," in *Eerdmans Dictionary of Early Judaism*, ed. J. J. Collins and D. Harlow (Grand Rapids: Eerdmans, 2010), 471–74.

17. On the Hebrew for "sign" of the covenant here, see אוֹת ("*ot*"), in *Concise Dictionary of Classic Hebrew*, ed. D. J. Clines (Sheffield: Sheffield Phoenix, 2009), 9.

18. It is noteworthy that the term "seal" (*sphragis*), used for Abraham's circumcision, is also used of the Holy Spirit for converts to the Christian faith in 2 Cor. 1:22 and Eph. 1:13 and 4:3. It is a very short step to move from the Holy Spirit to baptism, as we have shown.

19. Witherington, *Troubled Waters*, 114–15.

20. I am convinced this logic is also at work in Acts 2:39 as well as probably Rom. 4:11.

21. For special literature on these verses, see Paul D. Gardner, "'Circumcised in Baptism—Raised through Faith': A Note on Col 2:11–12," *Westminster Theological Journal* 45 (1983): 172–77. Besides the literature mentioned above, others challenges to infant baptism are offered by J. P. T. Hunt, "Colossians 2:11–12, the Circumcision/Baptism Analogy, and Infant Baptism," *Tyndale Bulletin* 42 (1990): 227–44; Jeffrey Peterson, "'The Circumcision of Christ': The Significance of Baptism in Colossians and the Churches of the Restoration," *Restoration Quarterly* 43 (2001): 65–77.

22. For a sketch of the relevant texts, see E. F. Ferguson, *The Early Church at Work and Worship*, vol. 2, *Catechesis, Baptism, Eschatology, and Martyrdom* (Eugene, OR: Cascade, 2014), 144–54.

23. Witherington, *Troubled Waters*, 86. I would not use "defunct" but "fulfilled." Witherington offers a mediating theory of dual baptism in which infant baptism is a legitimate deduction from New Testament theology as

well as possibly present in the New Testament. He focuses on baptism as a community event that points to the divine act of grace in Spirit baptism but at the same time has deep appreciation for credo-baptism. Dual-baptism theory, where one church will baptize either infants or adults upon profession of faith, has become more common; see Michael F. Bird, *Evangelical Theology: A Biblical and Systematic Introduction* (Grand Rapids: Zondervan, 2013), 768–71.

24. Bird, *Evangelical Theology*, 761. I prefer the term "fulfilled" instead of "replaced," which term also expresses how Bird discusses Col. 2:11–12 on pp. 761–62.

25. Bird, *Evangelical Theology*, 762.

26. For those who care about the technical meaning of "covenant theology," I am using this expression broadly and include Anglicans, but I am not restricting it to the Reformed, who make much of the covenant of works and the covenant of grace. For a good example of a Reformed covenant theology approach to infant baptism, one that does emphasize family, see Robert R. Booth, *Children of the Promise: The Biblical Case for Infant Baptism* (Phillipsburg, NJ: P&R, 1995).

27. No one has written more forcefully from this angle today than Catholic theologian Scott Hahn. See his *Kinship by Covenant: A Canonical Approach to the Fulfillment of God's Saving Promises*, Anchor Yale Bible Reference Library (New Haven: Yale University Press, 2009).

28. For a good discussion, see Witherington, *Troubled Waters*, 41–47.

29. A spouse made "holy" could well be connected to what is called a "licit" marriage in Jewish thinking, and thus the child being made "holy" follows that line of family thinking. For a very good discussion, see Roy E. Ciampa and Brian S. Rosner, *The First Letter to the Corinthians* (Grand Rapids: Eerdmans, 2010), 296–306.

30. John Calvin, *Institutes of the Christian Religion*, ed. John T. McNeill, trans. Ford Lewis Battles, Library of Christian Classics 20–21 (Philadelphia: Westminster, 1960), 2:1329 (4.16.6).

31. Bryan Chapell, *Why Do We Baptize Infants? Basics of the Faith* (Phillipsburg, NJ: P&R, 2006), 9–10.

32. Bird, *Evangelical Theology*, 765.

33. Garwood Anderson, in personal correspondence, has pointed me to another argument that is more complex but is worth sorting out quickly here: (1) In Galatians some are being accused of "works of the law" because of the issue of demanding circumcision for gentile believers. (2) In chapter 3 Paul teaches that they are incorporated into Christ *by baptism* (v. 27): "for all of you who were baptized into Christ have clothed yourselves with Christ." By baptism into Christ the gentile believers become children of Abraham (3:16, 29), not by circumcision. Hence, (3) it can be argued that in Gal. 3 Paul sees baptism as fulfilling the rite of circumcision for earliest Christianity.

Chapter 6: The Act of Baptism

1. Robin M. Jensen, *Baptismal Imagery in Early Christianity: Ritual, Visual, and Theological Dimensions* (Grand Rapids: Baker Academic, 2012), 17–20. For the Red Sea crossing, see 20–23.

2. Timothy George encourages Baptist churches to bring back the anointing with oil at baptism services. George, foreword to *Believer's Baptism: Sign of the New Covenant in Christ*, ed. Thomas R. Schreiner and Shawn D. Wright (Nashville: B&H, 2006), Kindle location 194.

3. I. H. Marshall, "The Meaning of the Verb 'Baptize,'" in *Dimensions of Baptism: Biblical and Theological Studies*, ed. Stanley Porter and Anthony R. Cross, Journal for the Study of the New Testament 234 (London: Sheffield Academic, 2002), 8–24.

4. Technical terms are often used in the literature: "immersion" for dunking, "perfusion" or "affusion" for pouring, and "aspersion" for sprinkling.

5. Didache 7.1–4.

6. "Chrism," which is consecrated oil, is a mixture of oil and balsam. It is sometimes called "myrrh."

7. J. I. Packer, *Baptism and Regeneration* (Newport Beach, CA: Anglican House, 2014), 16–17.

8. *Common Worship* here uses these words (found at the beginning of Holy Baptism in *The Book of Common Prayer*): "There is one Lord, one faith, one baptism: N and N [the names of those baptized], by one Spirit we are all baptized into one body." The response is this: "We welcome you into the fellowship of faith; we are children of the same heavenly Father; we welcome you."

Chapter 7: My Personal Testimony

1. William R. Estep, *The Anabaptist Story: An Introduction to Sixteenth-Century Anabaptism*, 3rd ed. (Grand Rapids: Eerdmans, 1996), 57–73.

2. For the story, see Estep, *Anabaptist Story*. For the theology of baptism among early Anabaptists, see Rollin Stely Armour, *Anabaptist Baptism: A Representative Study* (Scottdale, PA: Herald, 1966).

3. George R. Beasley-Murray, *Baptism in the New Testament* (Grand Rapids: Eerdmans, 1962); Geoffrey W. Bromiley, *Children of Promise—The Case for Baptizing Infants* (Grand Rapids: Eerdmans, 1979).

4. The issue, again, is whether baptism *actually does something to the child*. I believe it does.

5. Michael Green, *Baptism: Its Purpose, Practice, and Power* (Downers Grove, IL: InterVarsity, 1987), 53.

6. There are many books and studies on evangelicalism, but these three are standard explanations: George Marsden, *Understanding Fundamentalism and Evangelicalism* (Grand Rapids: Eerdmans, 1990); David W. Bebbington, *The Dominance of Evangelicalism: The Age of Spurgeon and*

Moody (Downers Grove, IL: IVP Academic, 2005); Randall Balmer, *Mine Eyes Have Seen the Glory: A Journey into the Evangelical Subculture in America*, 25th anniv. ed. (New York: Oxford University Press, 2014).

7. John R. W. Stott and J. Alec Motyer, *The Anglican Evangelical Doctrine of Infant Baptism* (London: Latimer Trust, 2008), 9.

8. Stott and Motyer, *Infant Baptism*, 16.

9. Stott and Motyer, *Infant Baptism*, 17.

10. Stott and Motyer, *Infant Baptism*, 20 (italics mine).

Scripture and Ancient Writings Index

Subject Index